£10

D1491887

THE DORAK AFFAIR

The
Dorak Affair

KENNETH PEARSON &
PATRICIA CONNOR

LONDON
MICHAEL JOSEPH

First published in Great Britain by
MICHAEL JOSEPH LTD
26 Bloomsbury Street
London, W.C.1
1967

© 1967 *by Kenneth Pearson and Patricia Connor*

Printed in Great Britain by
Western Printing Services Ltd, Bristol

'Archaeology is not a science,
it's a vendetta.'

Sir Mortimer Wheeler

CONTENTS

ILLUSTRATIONS

PREFACE

This book began in an innocent way: to describe one of the most important archaeological sites in the world, and the man who discovered it. It was not until we had been caught up in a gathering momentum of research that the story took on sinister aspects. By that time, curiosity to dig to the truth made it impossible to let go of the subject. For this reason it is important to record, in spite of allegations to the contrary, that it was we who set the wheels in motion, and not James Mellaart, the focal point of this investigation. But it is also important to record that without the co-operation of certain organs of the Turkish government, who may just as easily have slammed the door in the face of our enquiries, it would have proved impossible to move far along the route. We have in mind particularly Ankara's Ministry of Tourism, whose interpreters gave the most altruistic help, and its Ministry of Justice, who assisted our research in a way that would be inconceivable even in our own country.

We thought at this point, in order to help the reader with the pronunciation of a few names, of people and places, it would help to indicate how certain Turkish letters are spoken. Thus, c = j, ç = ch, ş = sh, ü = ue, ğ = an almost unpronounced y; so that Hasan Dağ is spoken Hasan Die, Çiğli (Chilly), Çatal Hüyük (Chatal Hueyuek) and Hacilar (Hajilar).

It only remains to express our gratitude to our own newspaper, the *Sunday Times*, and more specifically to Mr Godfrey Smith, the Editor of its Colour Magazine, who generously made possible this fuller account of a very puzzling story.

Patricia Connor
Kenneth Pearson
London
May, 1967

Chapter I

Encounter

The archaeologist sat uncomfortably at a corner table with his back to the wall; fair-haired, a stocky figure in a dark suit and a tartan tie, small eyes flickering behind horn-rimmed glasses, fingers fidgeting with knives and forks, patently tense.

He was sitting in Bertorelli's, a bourgeois Italian restaurant just north of Soho, where good solid food is served to businessmen and the fringe world of the arts. It is a sympathetic place to meet. Its waitresses, on nodding terms with a regular clientele, dump down their dishes unresentful that they will be eaten as an afterthought. There is no sense of that ritualised attendance on a table which stops conversation in its tracks. The restaurant's décor is unremarkable, the product of a series of accidents that combine to avoid distraction: it is brown, yellow and relaxing.

On Wednesday, 2 March, 1966, abandoning our car at a parking meter, we had climbed the stairs to one of Bertorelli's first-floor rooms, innocent of any drama but just aware of the nervousness that invests most first meetings. With us was James Mellaart, the archaeologist; British, well respected in his profession but as yet unknown outside it. So far our only contact had been on the telephone. Yes, he had said, he would be happy to talk over our project.

Public acceptance of archaeology is so conditioned by the familiar images of the Greek and Roman worlds that any discoveries revealing Man's first groping steps towards civilisation have the impact of news. Mellaart, an expert on the early cultures of Asia Minor, had been working for some time on an excavation in Turkey. By classical standards it was nothing more than a heap of earth on an ochre plain. It contained no soaring columns, no delicately carved stone, no intricate mosaic floors; but 8,000 years ago, on a site thirty-two acres in extent, a tribe of men, women and children had combined to subjugate their environment to a way of life unprecedented in history. Here, to take one example of their invention and expertise, Mellaart had dug up the world's first mirrors, polished chunks of volcanic glass shaped like half-oranges into which men could stare for the first time on an unrippled surface—and reflect. Perhaps then vanity was born. Greek and Roman ruins might epitomise more complex philosophies, but in Central Anatolia at least fifty-five centuries before Homer wrote of Troy, Man had begun to settle in mud huts and think. And Mellaart held the key to their inspiration. This was the reason for the lunch.

We ordered venison: it seemed an apt choice for an experimental encounter. And we ordered wine, lots of wine. We drank copiously and ate fitfully. And as we did so, on the other side of the table, Mellaart, tensions diminishing, gathered speed in conversation like an athlete heading for the long-jump. Dabbing at a sweating forehead, he launched into a description of his work at Çatal Hüyük with the mounting excitement of a man reporting directly from the battlefront; as if the experience was twenty-four hours old, not something observed across calendars of time.

He spoke a stream of words. 'Çatal Hüyük sticks up about sixty feet out of the Konya plain ... it's a plateau, really, ringed with extinct volcanoes. There are lots of mounds like it all over the place. Imagine what they might contain! This one stands by itself ... there's dust, my God the dust ... not many people, only peasants working in the fields. And a few storks. That's what it looks like now. It was a lot different then of course.' Mellaart began to define the region with a plate and a pepper-pot. His accent, betraying his birth in Holland, hovered near the sound made by an English-speaking Afrikaaner. 'You'd come out of the hills, covered with trees, to cross the plain. That'd be a fertile steppeland swarming with boar and wild asses. You'd probably avoid the forests—they'd be mixed oak and full of leopards, stags and giant cattle, until you came up against the river surrounding the city. That's where you'd stop. You'd find yourself faced with a line of blank walls . . . a rabbit warren of flat-topped houses . . . there were no doors or windows. You'd have to get in by the roof.'

The picture was compelling. Mellaart was using none of the qualifications that apply the brake to the lectures of so many indecisive academics. He did not allow his instincts to be disfigured by equivocation. He spoke with great assurance and authority, as if evidence, as yet uncovered, would one day prove him right beyond all denial. 'There are signs of a highly organised religious life. It's centred on fertility and the hunt. Their diet was well balanced . . . the teeth we found in the graves were in a condition you wouldn't find today. . . . Imagine what it must have been like for those hunters.' He had discovered a wild bull horn six feet long. 'Add two of those together, put a head in between, and you'll see why they painted giants like that on their temple walls. . . . Food supplies were pretty certain, sure enough, anyway, to enable specialist craftsmen to develop their arts and technology to an unprecedented level of sophistication. In fact, they'd already established the fundamental functions of town life . . . it might have been the cradle of civilisation.' And he spoke as if he had seen it happening.

Mellaart talked of himself as well. What had sparked him off to study archaeology? 'When I was eleven an uncle gave me a book . . . Breasted's book on Egypt . . . that was the beginning. And I saw a copy of the Rosetta Stone. It all came rushing in on me—Sumer, Crete, Mycenae. By the time I was twelve or thirteen I was looking at the pyramid texts in the original. And there was something called *The Tale of the Shipwrecked Sailor*, it's an Egyptian story written somewhere between 2000 and 1800 B.C. I'd bought a grammar and taught myself Ancient Egyptian.' By the time he was fourteen, Mellaart had added Ancient Greek and Latin to his languages. He seemed to swallow up and assimilate any new area of knowledge that got in the way between him and his objectives.

He went on; but we, separately, had made up our minds. There must be a large readership for this kind of subject: the beginnings of civilisation allied with a personality that seemed inspired whenever it touched on its passions. When was he returning to Turkey to dig again? In June. Could we come out at the end of the season, say in September, when he would undoubtedly have uncovered even more evidence for us to photograph? Of course, he said, he would be delighted to give us all the help he could. He was lecturing on Çatal Hüyük at the Institute of Archaeology in two weeks' time, perhaps we would like to hear what he had to say, especially as he would be using colour slides? We accepted and left the restaurant. On the windscreen of the car a traffic warden had stuck a two-pound fine. We had been in Bertorelli's for three hours.

At a quarter to six on the evening of Tuesday, 15 March, the Institute of Archaeology, filling one side of the many Bloomsbury squares occupying large areas of London University, was packed with a crowd of students and dons who struggled to find a seat in its lecture theatre. The entrance was jammed. In the corridor leading to it, Mellaart stood anxiously, smiling quickly at anyone he recognised. With him was his Turkish-born wife, Arlette, smaller than he, intensely dark-haired, with, too, a snatch of a smile. By six o'clock she was seated in the front row, hemmed in on both sides by a line of her compatriots: Turkish officials from the embassy, whose seats had been reserved for them. Their interest was purely cultural, or so it seemed. The lights went out, a coloured slide hit the screen, and Mellaart launched into a dazzling account of his discoveries in the season of 1965. 'It was a successful year,' he said. 'As you know, I was not allowed to dig the year before, but now our differences appear to be resolved.' Not allowed to dig in 1964? That was the first we had heard of it. Why? An answer would have to wait. Meanwhile, the lecture swept on. On the screen, exciting images followed hard on each other: necklaces, mirrors, wall paintings on which spindly Klee-like men leapt about in leopard loincloths around the giant bull, and only the occasional sight of a woman with a Mae West, hour-glass figure. And there were stately portraits of storks, a sign that even 8,000 years ago the people of Çatal Hüyük felt the same relationship to the bird as do the modern villagers. An hour later, Mellaart was wrapping up the lecture in a final burst of clipped, unchallengeable phrases. The lights flicked on, and the audience, momentarily blinded, exploded with applause. The Turks stayed on to congratulate the lecturer, and then left, solidly, like members of a football team.

The story, while we were tied up elsewhere professionally, stood still for the next four weeks; but then in the middle of April we phoned Mellaart once again to confirm his movements. The news was bad. It seemed unlikely, he said, that he would be given a permit to dig again. He offered no reason, no real reason, but murmured something about difficulties and that it was not unusual for the Turks to delay their decisions. We could see a good story on the brink of being snatched from us; after all, as yet, no one in the Western hemisphere had spelt out his discoveries in any detail. Perhaps the fact that our newspaper was interested might encourage the Turks to hurry matters along; we contacted the embassy in London and were passed on finally to Yusuf Mardin, the gentle, sympathetic chief of Turkish tourism in Britain. The ambassador, it appeared, had no wish to be involved. On Mardin's instructions we wrote to the Ministry of Tourism in Ankara, hoping, we said, that a permit would be given to Mellaart so that we might have more immediate reason for travelling to Turkey and writing of this 'cradle of civilisation'. In the middle of May, Mardin received a reply from the Turkish capital. He would not let us see the entire letter—it was confidential, but on the 28th he sent on one relevant section. It was an extract from the Ministry of Education, whose Department of Antiquities controls foreign excavation permits, to the Ministry of Tourism. It read:

'The excavations at Çatal Hüyük are being carried out by the British Institute of Archaeology (in Ankara). James Mellaart who previously worked on the diggings at Hacilar near Burdur, on their completion began work at Çatal Hüyük. The question of James Mellaart being granted permission to dig on the same site this year will be considered when his application is received. These excavations are in fact effected by a team which is appointed by the British Institute of Archaeology.

'The Ministry sees no reason why the *Sunday Times* should not write an article on the work . . . provided permission is granted by the Institute.'

The letter, in effect, said nothing. In fact, it raised more questions than it answered. If the Institute had to apply for a permit for Mellaart, why had it not done so? If this site held the key to one of the most important steps in Man's progress, why was work not being pressed on? Why had Mellaart made no mention at any of our meetings of the ritual through which he had to pass in order to dig? The archaeologist himself at least should know the answers. We rang him at his

house in St John's Wood. A woman came on at the other end
of the line. 'I'm sorry,' she said, 'but Mr Mellaart is not here.
He has gone to Turkey.'

As though a keystone had dropped out of an arch, weeks
of patient groundwork seemed on the point of collapse. Both
of us had spent a great deal of time studying the subject. We
had grown reasonably acquainted with the extent and significance of the Neolithic world and neither of us relished
abandoning the knowledge in a few well-filled notebooks.
But what was to be done next? The newspaper was ready to
print the story and neither of us felt inclined to let the opportunity slip. We turned to the one-time head of the British
Institute in Ankara, Professor Seton Lloyd, a colleague of
Mellaart's who had been his immediate chief in Turkey
some years before, and was now head of Western Asiatic
Archaeology in the Institute in London. We made an
appointment to see him in Bloomsbury.

Seton Lloyd epitomises the elderly English academic. He is
a tall, slim-boned man in his sixties, easily cast as a diplomat;
obviously, as an archaeologist, equally at home on an excavation, or administering from an office; never fired by a restless
ambitious drive, he is to be seen as a painstaking assembler
of facts, filling in, jigsaw fashion, pictures of prehistory; the
antithesis of Mellaart. We met on 2 June.

'You'd be surprised,' he said, 'if you knew what a handful Jimmie can be. You know, of course, about the
Toronto letter.' We did not. 'Oh, the man wrote an open
letter to the Royal Ontario Museum earlier in the year about
his season in '65. They'd been supporting him with money
and it's the sort of thing you're supposed to do in return. He
was talking about the Turks as Gestapo, spying on him and
all that. There was a Turkish archaeologist visiting New
York at the time and he got his hands on it. I expect he sent
it back to Ankara like a shot.' Could we see a copy of the
letter? Seton Lloyd thought not. 'It's marked "confidential"

and "not for publication".' In that case we would try to get a copy from Toronto, but if that failed, perhaps he might help us by letting us see his own? The professor said he would think about it. It was clear that he was seriously disturbed by the implications of the letter. He was, he said, waiting to set out soon on his own expedition to Lake Van in Eastern Turkey. 'So far I've had no reply to my application for a permit. And there are other British archaeologists waiting for theirs; no one's heard a thing from Ankara.' Did he connect this with Mellaart's action? The professor shrugged. 'But, of course,' he said, 'it all started with the Dorak treasure trouble. You know about that?' We stared blankly. 'Yes, the Turks think he was tied up with some treasure that was found in Izmir and then disappeared. They think it was smuggled out and Mellaart had a hand in it.' Did he know the precise details? 'Not exactly,' said Seton Lloyd, 'I can't remember it completely. But an account of the treasure was published in the *Illustrated London News* some years ago. Mellaart was supposed to have come across it in a house in Izmir. Through some Greek girl he was having a ding-dong with ... I think he was staying with her father.' Had the discovery been written up in any academic journals? We had found no sign of it. 'No,' said the professor. 'The trouble was there were no photographs, and no one is going to publish accounts of new finds unless there are photographs with them to substantiate the work. In the case of Dorak there were only some sketches that Jimmie made in the house.'

That afternoon we searched the files of the magazine, a publication which besides carrying news of the social scene gives a great deal of space to archaeological reports. There, in the issue for 29 November, 1959, was Mellaart's heavily illustrated four-page account of the find. The headline was unequivocating. 'The Royal Treasure of Dorak—a first and exclusive report of a clandestine excavation which led to the most important discovery since the Royal Tombs of Ur.' A series of striking pictures followed: five-inch-high statues of a goddess and her handmaidens, she with her hands supporting naked breasts, and all decorated with gold and silver ornaments; jewelled bracelets, ceremonial axeheads and sceptres in marble, lapis lazuli, obsidian, amber and gold; a two-handled drinking vessel in fluted gold; a re-creation of a woven rug on which a king lay in the tomb and which, said the report, had disintegrated as the grave was opened; and a dozen or so swords and daggers. They were, said the account, the contents of two royal tombs found on a hill near the village of Dorak, on the southern shore of Lake Apolyont, south of the Sea of Marmara, and excavated between 1919 and 1922 during the Turko-Greek war. One other artifact appeared to date the tomb as though the day of its completion had been chiselled on the door. Fragments of a sheet of gold which once covered a wooden throne were covered with hieroglyphics. Translated, they showed that the throne must have been a gift of the Pharaoh Sahure who lived between 2487 and 2473 B.C. This evidence, Mellaart stated in his report, was the first to show contact between the seafaring population of North-West Anatolia and Egypt of the Third Millennium. The tombs were relics of the Yortan culture, belonging to a neighbour state of Troy.

Where, then, was the treasure now? Inquiries revealed that since Mellaart's report, no sign of it had turned up anywhere in the world. If it had been smuggled from Turkey, no recognised museum owned it. Perhaps, as is all too frequent, it was buried in the secret vaults of some eccentric millionaire. Or did it in fact exist? Archaeological forgeries are not unprecedented, and one can imagine thwarted ambition twisting a scientific mind. Was Mellaart such a man? The propositions were now too numerous to be ignored. Mellaart, it was clear, was being prevented from further exploring his 'cradle of civilisation', an excavation that had won the unstinted applause of the world's archaeologists. There was no doubt of Çatal Hüyük's authenticity. But why the ban? Had his Toronto letter wounded the Turks irrevocably? Or did it in some way confirm their suspicions of a man who, they thought, was connected with the vanished Dorak hoard?

In the next three weeks pressure at a personal and editorial level for us to discontinue our inquiries grew intense. Archaeologists connected with the Institutes in both London and Ankara tried to dissuade us from our investigation. Did we not realise, they said, that by digging up this story we might affect Turkish attitudes to all British archaeologists? None of them as yet had received a permit for the coming season and our actions could hardly be a help. All of them missed the point. Mellaart was either a thief; in which case his exposure would surely isolate the blame that, as the Turks might see it, was now attached to them all. Or he was innocent; in which case someone in Ankara might be generous enough to allow him to return to Çatal Hüyük. They were unimpressed.

Of all the personalities involved, Mellaart seemed the least concerned at our interest. By now we had established contact with him at his Turkish home on the Bosphorus, and in a series of letters he and his wife made it clear that we would be welcome to question them as freely as we wished. They would, they said, give us all the time we needed. The Turkish press had been running stories about the 'ban', connecting it directly with the Toronto letter; and it appeared, from the tone of their notes that the Mellaarts, exhausted by the weight of accusations, were prepared at last to unburden themselves to uncommitted journalists. And we *were*, despite later allegations, uncommitted. 'Mellaart the Smuggler' and 'Mellaart the Victim' were equally good as headlines.

Just how complex a personality motivated Mellaart was made clear from his letter to the Royal Ontario Museum. By early June, Professor Seton Lloyd had agreed to lend us his copy of the document since none was obtainable from Toronto. It was not, to say the least, calculated to endear the Turks to its author. It was couched in terms violent enough to cause even the most outspoken diplomat to shudder. Speaking of the 1964 ban, Mellaart had written:

'A change of the Director General of Antiquities allowed certain xenophobic elements aided by the gutter press and the Cyprus crisis of 1964 to put strong pressure to bear on the Department and through envy and jealousy our application for a dig-permit for Çatal Hüyük was refused. "Western cultural imperialism" as it was called by the then Minister of Education was thwarted at least temporarily. . . .'

Further on in the letter, which for the most part was a deeply detailed account of his 1965 season, Mellaart grew more reckless. '. . . finally we had not less than five people to spy on us; two servants planted on us as agents provocateurs, a Museum guard on the site with the manners of a Gestapo man, the official government representative and an assistant representative to check on his colleague. Not a week passed without some intrigue. In this cloak and dagger atmosphere we started our fourth season of excavation, perhaps the most rewarding yet . . .'

Intensely chauvinistic as they are, sensitive to all shades of international opinion like a child that seeks nothing but acclaim from its elders, the Turks, on first glance, had every reason to feel offended, even if Mellaart's accusations had a basis in fact. It remained for us to confront him with his indiscretion. There must be some coherent explanation for such an outburst, and for the disappearance of the Dorak treasure. We made one last call to Ankara, to the British Institute of Archaeology, to enquire if at the last minute Mellaart had been granted his permit. The phone was answered by the Institute's secretary, Ferdinand La Grange. No, there was no one in the office. In that case, did he know . . . The question was chopped off in the air. From then on the line was filled with a non-stop, near-hysterical welter of words. Obviously, the wires between London and the Turkish capital had been humming. 'Why don't you leave us alone. . . . I know all about you. . . . You've no idea, my dear chap, what you are doing. . . . Nothing will please the Turks. . . . You don't know what damage you'll do to us. . . . That man has caused more trouble than . . .' The line was fading. We said thank you and hung up.

On 8 July we left for Istanbul.

Chapter 2

Istanbul: The Trail Begins

The airport bus plunged along the dual-carriage highway towards Istanbul, overtaking a flock of sheep heading with the stream. It swept past rusty fields dotted with shanty-town huts, huge pyramids of melons by the roadside, to slip suddenly into the city itself through a great crumbling gash in towering Byzantine walls. It swerved down broad boulevards between growing concrete and glass, a façade for dirt or cobbled lanes with shabby tenements leaning on each other for support, and twisted its way through a complex of new crossroads, where archaeologists dig within inches of the traffic to unearth one more column of the Roman Empire. Beneath an emperor's aqueduct, a modern under-pass dives through the roots of ruins. Past an elephantine mosque and into the centre of town, the bus edged across the Atatürk Bridge over the Golden Horn; shimmering glimpses of a jumble of centuries: bleached American cars scarred by collision, women in baggy trousers, a dress from a boutique, bank signs on every corner, water sellers, overloaded lorries grinding from the quaysides, and an old man weighed down like a packhorse with a trembling chest of drawers. Along the Istiklâl, crowds saunter by cosmopolitan shops, steaming snack bars and cinemas selling Ottoman epics, the cowboy films of Asia Minor. Scarlet gladioli. And rows of shoe-shine boys in Taksim Square, squatting over footrests decorated like portable Renaissance altars with polished brass and coloured fairy stories.

Our base was the Park Hotel, forecourt jammed with cars, number plates ranging from the familiar marks of Britain to the Arabic insignia of Egypt. The foyer was faded elegance, space and marble floors. By nightfall, the hotel was hanging over the Bosphorus like a theatre balcony. And on the terrace, the city's café society moved among its tables, cocktails and gossip, journalists, actors, businessmen and a few burnt-eyed women. Occasionally, a group stopped talking, seduced into silence by the view. The scene, quite quickly, was bled of its rainbow colours until a blue wash covered the land, and only shape began to dominate the eye. The minarets of St Sophia and the Blue Mosque soared above the tangled alleys of Old Stamboul like black daggers. Beneath them, the Golden Horn turned silver. Across the Bosphorus, Asia, a mile and a half away, faded into the darkness, while ferry boats like water beetles scurried on their last clear-sighted runs before switching on beams of light to feel their way to Üsküdar and back.

Down in the street at the back of the hotel, a tattered saloon slid to a halt by the doors of a mosque. Out of it leapt a 'mod' muezzin. He raced up the spiral staircase to the balcony of the minaret, and in a wailing, sing-song voice that grew more beautiful as it became familiar, he called the faithful to prayer. All over the city, in tiny echoes, Allah was being praised.

The next morning, Saturday, 9 July, we reported to the headquarters of the Ministry of Tourism to collect our foreign press cards. To travel without them, we were to discover, might be hazardous. We waited briefly, sipping small glasses of weak tea in an outer office. A door opened and a tall, slim civil servant entered. 'Ah, Mr Pearson and Miss Connor.' He laughed at our surprise. We were there, we thought, unannounced. 'It's all right,' he said, 'I have your cards with your photographs on my desk. I am Rüknettin Bey. How can I help you?' We explained that we should need interpreters everywhere our story took us in Turkey, and he assured us this would be done. 'I shall write at once to Ankara and warn them.' We thanked him, drank more tea and left.

The Bosphorus is Turkey's main street, connecting the Sea of Marmara with the Black Sea eleven miles to the north-east. Its banks, crowded with villas and villages are linked by a service of ferry boats plying directly between Europe and Asia, or zig-zagging from shore to shore with passengers and cargo.

That afternoon we caught the 3.38 from Beşiktaş, a suburb of Istanbul. Our destination was Kanlica, where, on a night out, young Turks stop off to eat its special yoghourt. For us it meant the first meeting in Turkey with Mellaart, who lives there in the summer in a house owned and inhabited by his wife's parents. For the best part of an hour, the boat cruised gently from stop to stop past Ottoman palaces, whose harems are now museums, and wooden multi-storeyed buildings resembling a trial run for Venice.

Seven miles up the Bosphorus, on the Asiatic shore, we disembarked to meet Mellaart waiting on the pier. We strolled a hundred yards to a door in a high wall on the edge of the village, beyond which lay a garden in full flower. It looked English, with dahlias, roses, clematis, irises and petunias; but flourishing among these were plants that contradicted a first impression. Coral trees, pomegranates and pavlonia grew by the water's edge on a private quayside. A long table was laid for tea in shade, beside which stood a white-jacketed servant. Arlette Mellaart came from the house, smiling warmly.

'I am sorry,' she said, 'but two Frenchmen have just turned up. They're from television. They've come to do a film on Jimmie.' She caught a look of dismay. With so much time and money about to be invested in research, the shores of the Bosphorous were no place to discover that others were already sniffing the scent in the air. 'Don't worry,' said Arlette, 'they are here purely for archaeology.'

It seemed so. Across the garden, the two men were taking pictures of the plaster cast of a mother goddess of Çatal Hüyük, a Neolithic op-art figure with a belly ringed with concentric circles. It was not so strange that they should be there. An awareness of Mellaart's work in Turkey was growing both in Britain and in France, and although we did not know it at the time, it had suddenly appeared worthy of examination in America. A third interested party was soon to descend on Mellaart from Washington.

In Kanlica, the archaeologist himself presented a picture somewhat different from his London image. The tension was still there, just discernible in his sudden gestures. But dressed in open-necked summer rig, he seemed expanded. If his interior solitude was still to be seen, it was only when he detached himself from a group to stand alone on the quay-side, staring into the water, puffing on a cigarette like a young girl.

The house itself stood on the south side of the garden. It was an eighteenth-century timber mansion with a jutting upper storey supported by upward curving beams, looking like a cross between a giant Kentish barn and the stern of a Spanish galleon. Its marble foyer divided the interior into two sections, once inhabited by segregated male and female communities. The rooms which led off the entrance hall sloped and twisted with the collapse of old age. Mellaart's study overlooked the quayside, and was the most revealing room in the house. Turkish rugs covered the floor. A long kitchen table was littered with piles of papers in the middle of which sat a respectable but ancient Remington typewriter. Lying around were scores of books on archaeology and *The Treasury of Flowers and Plants*. To one side of the table, pinned to the wall, was a Scottish National Trust brochure, *The Raising of the Standard*, recounting the tragic exploits of Bonny Prince Charlie in 1745. On a side table was a heap of Gaelic records. The top two were called 'Orain Ne Gaidhealtachd' and 'Songs of Gaeldom'. On the inside of a wooden cabinet, Mellaart had stuck a portrait of the Queen.

At dinner that night, as we sank the raki in the bottle, Mellaart, eating in the lee of passing ships, was in good humour. His best jokes he told in a Scottish accent, mimicking a thin Highland voice . . . 'If the soup had been as hot as the wine, if the wine had been as old as the turkey, if the turkey had had breasts like the waitress, it would have been a decent meal.'

It was midnight when we broke away from the scene: water lapping against the terrace, thin jazz sounds floating across the Bosphorus from nightclubs on the other side, the occasional thrash of a ship's propellor, the warmth of the Turkish wine. We had missed the last boat for Istanbul, and caught, instead, a taxi for Üsküdar, which rattled at breakneck speed along the winding shore road to the south. On the radio Tom Jones was singing 'What's New Pussycat?' The driver, seeming to think it was our national anthem, turned the volume to full. A satisfactory night; but for one thing. The word 'Dorak' had not been mentioned.

The next morning, in his study, Mellaart began his story. He was a descendant, he said, of the Macdonalds of the Isles; more particularly of the Maclarty's, a sect of the clan. In the seventeenth century, the family had had to flee to Holland. 'That's where my name "Maclarty" was changed in the Dutch to "Mellaart". It's a sort of latinised version.

'I was at school in Holland when the Germans invaded it. But I stayed there. . . . I had Dutch papers as well as British. But when I was eighteen, that'd be in 1944, that's when things got tricky. The Germans could have called me up. So I went to the Swiss consul—he was looking after British affairs, and I told him I wasn't going to work for the Nazis. What could I do? He told me not to go home. The Gestapo might be looking for me. . . . He got me a job in the museum at Leiden. I hid myself in the Egyptology department, mending broken pots.

'After the war,' he went on, 'I stayed in Leiden, waiting for a university place in England, and I got to University College in London eventually. They didn't run a course in archaeology, so I had to do Egyptology and read archaeology on the side. . . . There was some sort of muddle at the time.' Mellaart laughed. 'I was put on a post-graduate course by the professor there . . . a Czech . . . Yaroslav Crny . . . that was him. He wasn't very good at regulations. One day my tutor went to see him about a degree. "A degree," he said, "but Mellaart's a doctor, no? No? But he should have been a doctor years ago."'

Mellaart was not being immodest. From the evidence, it is clear that he is no ordinary plodding digger. He has the gift, a colleague said, of 'a water diviner'. The envious call him 'lucky'. But it is not luck that has made him successful. While others may work on sites with very little unearthed to their credit, Mellaart has the knack of walking a site for hours, picking a spot to excavate, and striking it rich almost at once.

He reads signs like a Sherlock Holmes. A slight depression thrown into relief by the setting sun at Jericho led him once to rich graves and forty intact vases before breakfast. He found the only Iron Age brooch on an otherwise unproductive hill fort in Herefordshire. And there was the occasion in Cyprus when, because he could not afford the fare, he turned down a team outing into town and stayed instead on the site. That Saturday afternoon, alone, he uncovered a Mycenaean bronze hoard.

On the day Mellaart finished his finals at University College in 1951, he set out for the British Institute in Ankara with a scholarship. He was glad to have won it. It would give him a chance to explore a theory that had arisen from his Egyptian studies. About the thirteenth century B.C., an almost mythical race known as the Sea People, part-pirates who sailed the Eastern Mediterranean, had annihilated the armies of many civilisations until their progress was halted by the Egyptians in a great and definitive battle. Archaeologists hold several theories about their origins. Perhaps, thought Mellaart, the Sea People had been based on the shores of Asia Minor. Perhaps proof was there to be discovered.

Peasants harvesting in Central Anatolia in the early 1950s would have been aware from time to time of an odd figure trudging the distant dirt roads. The man was dressed in baggy trousers, a khaki shirt and gym shoes. He carried a rucksack on his back and his pockets were full of stones which he hurled at inquisitive sheep dogs. It was Mellaart; sharing rooms with Turks to save money in Çumra, Karaman and Can Hasan, criss-crossing the Konya Plain from these local towns, plotting prehistoric mounds on ancient maps. He plodded along until holes appeared in his soft-soled shoes or the first winter snows drove him back to Ankara. And he was stretching his one-year scholarship of £350 to keep him going for two. Seton Lloyd, his chief at that time in Ankara, remembers him as 'my scruffy little assistant'.

Even then, he was pursuing clues like a relentless bloodhound. He discovered his first Neolithic site at the Turkish village of Hacilar by tracing local gossip to a nearby coffee house and a chauffeur by the name of Şevket Çetinkaya, who, with some prompting, produced two strangely decorated pots from his house. The trail finally took him to a field beneath a rock bluff and alongside an orchard where a village dating back to 7000 B.C. lay buried under the crops. The discovery marked the first step in the growth of Mellaart's reputation, and the beginnings of Şevket's climb to becoming a millionaire.

But if the archaeologist showed excitement at unearthing Hacilar, it was nothing compared with what was to follow at Çatal Hüyük. Mellaart, sitting on the quayside at Kanlica, recalled the discovery with passion, the faint traces of a Dutch accent hardening as he recollected his first emotions.

'It was about four in the afternoon . . . 10 November, 1958, it was . . . when we arrived at the mound. I had two friends with me. And a whopping great mound it was. We'd only seen it from the road before. . . . My friends walked to the top. I stayed at the bottom looking at the ground. Imagine it! I picked up a bag of pottery and about a dozen arrowheads . . . obsidian they were . . . within the first few minutes. On top of that, I could see traces of burnt walls on the west side of the tell. That's the side swept by the wind. They formed a rectangular pattern. That meant only one thing—there were houses galore.

'Suddenly, I heard a shout from the top. My two friends were racing down. They were shouting, "It's Neolithic at the top". And I shouted back, "My God. It's bloody Neolithic at the bottom as well".'

Mellaart had in front of him a sixty-foot layer of a Late Stone Age civilisation. And although he was going to have to wait three years for permission to dig there, at least he knew at that moment that the site was almost bound to offer up new evidence on the cultural development of Man.

'It was getting dark by now,' said Mellaart, 'but it was hard to tear ourselves away. Anyway, we couldn't see much more, so we went back to the nearest town and the three of us rented a room meant for six. There was no lock, and we wanted to keep the place to ourselves, so we took the handle off the door. And we got bloody drunk.'

They left early the next morning, hangovers and all, paid a brief visit to Çatal Hüyük ('just to make sure it was still there') and then returned to Ankara. Back at the hotel a minor panic was rumbling. No one could get into the room.

On the terrace of a house on the Bosphorus, James Mellaart
entertains and writes while banned from digging at Çatal

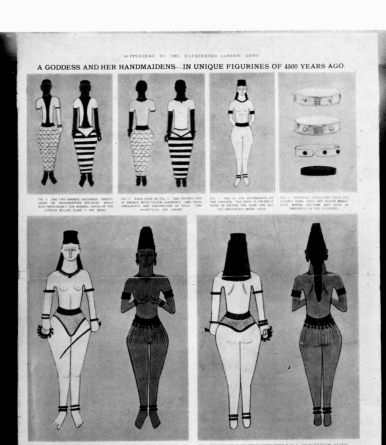

A page from the *Illustrated London News* of 29 November 1959, an issue of the magazine which carried Mellaart's first account of the Dorak discovery and upset Ankara

Mellaart, dreaming out of the window on the north-bound train, still had the door-knob in his pocket.

Mellaart broke off his story to go into the house to change. He was due to lecture that night at the British consulate in Istanbul. He reappeared ten minutes later in the garden, pacing nervously, smoking furiously, wearing a dark blue suit and the inevitable tartan tie. That tie is a brand image. He clings to the Scottish elements in his existence, and he has even been known to lecture in a kilt. It seems to shut out his life in Holland.

The lecture, as usual, had been a great success, and the cocktail party was in full swing. The guests were predominantly English: large women in flower print frocks and caved-in men in limp oatmeal linen jackets and old school ties. High-pitched voices fluttered through the giant consulate building which had known its days of power-driven action when, before the Turks moved their capital to Ankara, it had been the British Embassy.

Through the charm, the courtesy and the good breeding, nervous warnings edged to the surface. 'I know of course, old boy, you'll be very careful when you write your piece about Jimmie.' ... 'Do you think you're doing the wise ... er ... mm?' ... 'I say, I hear you're going to Ankara. Nice place. Treat the whole thing delicately, won't you?'

A Turkish professor of archaeology deplored the ban on his friend. Matters could be difficult in jealous academic worlds. He himself had been invited to contribute a volume on Anatolia to a world-famous series being published in Geneva. A request, one would have thought, that might excite the admiration of his colleagues and countrymen. Envy seemed to be the main reaction.

'All I wanted to do,' he said, 'was to take pictures for my book in the museum in Ankara. What happens? They tell me I cannot plug in my lights. The electricity is not working.

Of course, it work. A friend, he tell me they give orders that it must not be switched on.' He shrugs. 'If they do that to me, a foreigner . . .'

From across the room Arlette Mellaart waved. With her was a slightly-built, shy Turkish woman, Nemeka Altan, the government representative on Mellaart's last season at Çatal Hüyük. Why, we asked her, did she think the archaeologist has been refused permission to dig?

She answered quickly in Turkish, her voice a soft murmur; we waited to hear the translation. Suddenly, out of the babble of words, one leapt up loud and clear: 'Dorak.'

Arlette turned and smiled. 'But of course, you know all about the Dorak business. We'll talk about it tomorrow.'

On Wednesday, 13 July, over lunch in the garden at Kanlica, Mellaart began his story of the Dorak treasure. We were to take him over the same ground several times in the next few days. On each occasion the details remained substantially the same. There were minor discrepancies, but as Mellaart said himself, 'It was eight years ago'.

'I was going down to Izmir by train. I wanted to complete a survey of potential sites I'd been doing down there. Early in the summer of 1958, I think it was.' Arlette Mellaart consulted a pile of diaries and confirmed the year.

'We were getting near the coast, and it was getting dark. My compartment started to fill up, so I moved further down the train to an empty one. Soon after that, a girl came in and sat down opposite me. She was very attractive . . . in a tarty sort of way.' Arlette smiled.

'But the thing that made me stare was what she was wearing on her wrist. She had a solid gold bracelet. It looked prehistoric. I said I was an archaeologist and asked her if I could have a look at it. It was the kind of thing that had only been found at Troy. She said she'd got lots like it at home, and asked if I would like to see them. Well, you know, it sounded important. I said I would.

'By the time we arrived in Izmir, it was very dark. I don't remember the way we went very clearly. But I know we took a taxi to a quay, and caught a ferry boat across the bay to Karşiyaka. That's a district on the other side. And got another taxi from there to her house.

'It was very old, with two or three floors, I should think. Inside, we talked for a bit and then she asked me if I would like to stay to dinner.'

'When did you get to see the rest of the stuff?'

'While we were eating, she began to show me one or two things. They were in a chest of drawers, lying on cotton wool. They must have been there some time, they were very dusty... I don't think they'd been looked after at all well. The things were mostly broken. All the metal was corroded. The gold, of course, still looked the same.'

'Did she get it all out at once?'

'No, that's the funny thing. She seemed to be teasing me. I was afraid to ask too many direct questions in case she got afraid and stopped the whole thing.'

'What did you identify them as?'

'Well, there were a couple of faded photographs of skele-tons in the tombs. There were two tombs. A king, I suppose, in one; and the queen in the other. The pictures were charred at the edges. And there were some notes in Greek. Modern Greek. Some of those were burnt round the edges as well.'

'What kind of notes were they?'

'I think they must have been written by some sort of an archaeologist. They were very scientific. There was a sketch map of the find. It looked as if the things had been dug up when the Greeks occupied that part of Turkey just after the first world war, near a village called Dorak.'

'What about getting pictures of the treasure?'

'I hadn't got my camera with me. It was broken and I'd left it behind. So I asked her if I could get someone in to take some pictures. "No," she said, "but I'll send you some later." I don't think she wanted anyone else to see the stuff. I think she was afraid.

'Anyway, by this time it had got very late and she said I could stay the night if I was so interested.'

Mellaart, in fact, stayed three or four nights, drawing details of the artifacts, making rubbings of the hieroglyphics, and transposing the notes with the help of the girl into a lengthy commentary.

'Was there anyone else in the house?" we asked.

'I'm sure there was an old man in one of the rooms,' said Mellaart. 'I had an idea it might have been her father. I never saw him. And there might have been an old woman in the kitchen helping with the cooking. I just had the feeling she was there.'

'What did the house look like inside?'

Mellaart took a scrap of paper and began to sketch an out-line of the first floor. 'I was given a small bedroom in the corner here, next to the dining-room. It had a balcony and that overlooked a garden at the side and round the back. I don't remember much more.'

'Didn't you go out?'

'No.'

'Not at all? Not even for cigarettes?'

'No, she went out for me ... I didn't want to waste a minute. I had the feeling that she might get scared and stop what I was doing.'

'What kind of a girl was she?'

'About twenty or twenty-one. She spoke English with an American accent. That's why I thought she might have been connected with the Americans.'

'And her name?'

'Well, I realised just as I was leaving that I'd only been calling her Anna. I left very early in the morning to catch a train and I still couldn't see where I was, so I asked her her name and address. She said, "Anna Papastrati and it's 217 Kazim Dirik street".'

By 3.30 that afternoon, we had moved out of the heat on the terrace and into the study. Mellaart sat in the chair by his typewriter, beads of sweat shining on his face.

'Of course,' said Arlette, 'ever since, the newspapers here have been attacking Jimmie. It's hardly a coincidence, but every year we come back here, there's some new attack in the papers. Now it's the Toronto letter. I know it was stupid to send it . . .'

'Any bloody fool would know that you don't publish that sort of thing,' Mellaart broke in angrily. 'I'd sent it to a friend expecting he would cut out those personal bits, but he was away and someone else just went ahead and printed the whole thing. Get the cuttings out, Arlette, and let them see what bloody lies the papers write.'

Arlette went to the wooden cabinet and abstracted a large file of papers. On the top was a cutting which suggested that because of the letter, Mellaart was being investigated with the idea that he would be declared *persona nongrata* in Turkey. But what was even more interesting was the compact bunch of clippings in the middle of the file. They told their own story.

On 29 May, 1962, *two and a half years* after the Dorak discovery had broken in the *Illustrated London News*, Turkey's second leading national newspaper, *Milliyet* ('Nationality'), with a circulation of 200,000, had launched a three-day campaign against Mellaart.

On the first day, across all eight columns of page one, the banner headline exclaimed: 'An Historic Royal Treasure Worth a Milliard Lire Smuggled Out.' The value of the hoard—£48 million—was ludicrous. The story itself was the result of an interview with Mellaart, conducted, according to the archaeologist, on the lines of 'how interesting this all is'.

There had been no hint of venom in the encounter. On the second day, 30 May, still with a front-page story, Dorak villagers were quoted as describing 'a fair-haired, fat, middle-aged foreigner' who was seen near the tombs with a woman either in 1955 or 1956. On 31 May, Mellaart was still page one news. A new photograph showed 'a youth of Mustafakemal-pasha' (a town near Dorak) who had come forward as a result of the first day's story to identify Mellaart as a man he had seen in town about the dates mentioned. The implications seemed irrefutable: Mellaart had dug up the treasure himself. But who was the woman? Arlette Mellaart or Anna Papastrati or someone else? Either Mellaart was lying or he had a cast-iron case for libel against *Milliyet*.

What had Mellaart done about it? 'I took advice from my friends, English and Turkish. They all said the same thing: "It's best to forget about it. The Turkish newspapers are always doing this. It'll soon die down."' But by now the Turkish Press in general had the taste of blood in its mouth, and from *Milliyet*'s campaign on was to attach Mellaart's name, directly or obliquely, to almost any story that involved the disappearance of antiquities.

Put into an historical perspective, the state of the Turkish Press was to be viewed with sympathy. As the voice of an emerging nation, for years it had been subjected to strong government control. More recently, as the country's leaders felt a greater sense of security, so its Press had been given its head. Its reaction was typical: it began to interpret its new-found freedom as a licence to print supposition as fact. Mellaart was just another of its victims. Nevertheless, *Milliyet*'s story had contained one indisputable fact. When the authorities, sprung into action by the Dorak revelation in London, started to investigate its details, they discovered a vital clue was missing. Both Anna Papastrati and her house had vanished.

.   .   .

First thing the next morning, Thursday, 14 July, we were in touch through our interpreter with Rüknettin Bey at the Ministry of Tourism. Would he, we asked, arrange an interview in the *Milliyet* office with Turhan Aytul, the reporter who had written the Mellaart story. We needed, we said, to check his facts. Of course, said the officials at the Ministry, we will keep in touch. It was a frustrating day. Hour by hour the news was less than helpful. The lines to the newspaper office were busy. The editor was in conference. The director who could really handle our request was unfortunately away. It was not, unhappily, the right day of the week.

Our time, however, was not wasted. For the first three hours of the day we shopped in Istanbul's Covered Bazaar, a city of stores, some no bigger than a wardrobe, reached through a warren of alleys under vaulted stone roofs. At intersections, men and boys washed their faces and their feet in fountains. In its auction rooms, dealers bid for carpets or jewels. Competition was sharp. There was a price to be ignored and a value to be haggled over. We were not shopping for local needlework, but for Neolithic pottery.

In the Bedestan section of the bazaar, where the antique merchants cluster, within an hour we had been offered, among the pedestrian Greek and Roman souvenirs, antiquities three times their age and six times their worth. Outside, where the Armenians sell and barter, where the word 'Neolithic' has to be whispered, the goods are locked in safes, wrapped in newspaper. In a shop eight feet square, a dealer and his assistant produced a Hacilar goddess that was going for £110.

'We have to be very careful,' said the young English-speaking assistant. 'We are not supposed to have these things. They should be in the museums.' But if we bought it, we said, how would we get it out of the country?

'Oh, that's easy,' he answered, 'we can send it through the post. It goes out through the American Army Post Office in Izmir. Their things don't have to go through the Customs.' He was an extremely helpful young man, who had learnt his English in Basingstoke. 'If you leave your name and address in America,' he said, mistaking our identity, 'I can always send you an illustrated brochure whenever anything else like this comes along. We get a good supply.'

It was clear that whatever opinion the Turkish newspapers might have of Mellaart, the illicit market had sources closer to home. Real or fake, a stream of artifacts was being fed through Istanbul's bazaar to tourists and large-scale international dealers alike.

By four o'clock that afternoon, direct action seemed the only course. If we could not seduce *Milliyet* into an interview, rape was the alternative. Our interpreter, accustomed to the formalities of Middle Eastern diplomacy, was horrified. Nevertheless, we were there. We were directed to the office of *Milliyet*'s foreign news editor, where his assistant, Mehmet Ali Birand, well known among Western diplomatic correspondents, a tall, handsome figure, young, bi-lingual and sympathetic, acted as his paper's advocate. The reporter Turhan Aytul was called in with his file. He was a slight, dark haired character, wearing glasses, with his shirt sleeves rolled up. The cross-examination began.

'Why did the story take two and a half years to travel from London to Istanbul?'

He did not know, but a friend had given him the article torn out of the *Illustrated London News*.

'Which friend?'

He would not say.

'A friend in Ankara?'

He would not say.

'Do you remember the picture you ran on the second day with the peasants standing in a grave?'

'Yes,' he said, producing the original sepia print.

'Was it taken when you went to Dorak to investigate?'

'Yes.'

'Do you suppose the sides of the grave would have stayed as clean cut as that for seven years since 1955 when Mellaart, according to you, dug there? Do you believe that a king would have been buried in a grave only two feet deep?"

'I don't know,' he said, 'I'm not an archaeologist.'

'Do you think peasants can remember accurately someone they saw years before?"

'They can, if they've been paid.' It was not too clear at that point whether he meant by Mellaart or by himself.

'If Mellaart was supposed to be in Dorak in 1955 or 1956, how do you account for the fact that he has an alibi? That there are several people, English and Turk, who know where he was those years? And it was 300 miles south of Dorak?'

'I don't need alibis. He was also seen in Dorak. After my first article a boy from Mustafakemalpasha came forward and said he recognised Mellaart from the picture. Let me ask you a question. Why did the address he gave to the Department of Antiquities not exist? I offered to pay his fare to Izmir to show me the house. But he would not go. This is not the sign of an innocent man.'

We conceded the point. But detail by detail, Turhan Aytul was taken through his notes. In the main he stuck to his story, but his notes covering the dates during which the peasants were supposed to have seen their foreigner stated clearly 'between 1953 and 1955'. The dates in the paper—1955 or 1956—must, Aytul said, have been a misprint.

'Perhaps,' we asked, 'you can tell us how this purely hypothetical value of £48 million was written into your headline?'

The reporter looked puzzled. 'A sub-editor must have done it,' he said, pointing to an *Illustrated London News* caption. This, he thought, was the source. The date 'the third millennium B.C.' had been translated, by what system of calculation cannot be imagined, into 'one milliard lire'.

Elsewhere, whenever he was stuck for an answer through two and a half hours of questioning, despite the presence of two interpreters, he retired behind his lack of English or said, 'Only Mellaart has the key'.

As we left the office, thinking perhaps that Turhan Aytul was genuinely motivated by a concern for the way in which Turkey was being robbed of its heritage, Mehmet Ali Birand said, 'I am not so convinced about Mellaart's guilt as I was when we began.'

'Why did you refuse to go to Izmir with Turhan Aytul?' we asked Mellaart the next day.

'It's the first I've heard of the offer,' he said.

'How can you ever expect people to believe it existed?'

'Ask my father-in-law. He believes me.'

Kadri Cenani, Arlette Mellaart's father, a descendant of a line of Grand Viziers to the Sultan, is today a vice-president of the Turkish Press Association and a public relations consultant with Shell; but these modern roles sit strangely on this diplomat of the *ancien régime*. His own rooms in the house at Kanlica are lined with silver-framed photographs of visiting royalty of the nineteenth century. Their signatures tell the story of politics conducted at the personal level of aristocratic rulers. He speaks English and French as fluently as he speaks Turkish; his own daughter did not learn the language of her country until she was fourteen.

'In the spring of 1964 I sent a registered envelope to Anna Papastrati at 217 Kazim Dirik street,' explained Cenani, 'I registered it because in this way the Post Office would have to account for it. It was returned to me marked: "The addressee was asked for at 217 Kazim Dirik street but the above-named was unknown there." So you see I knew a house existed at that address.'

Kadri Cenani had also at the same time contacted, through acquaintances in the Turkish Cabinet, the Chief of Police at Izmir, Hüseyin Taluy.

'Taluy,' said Cenani, 'put his best man on the job. An inspector called *Başkomisar* Yilmez Çapin, head of the department for drug-trafficking, smuggling and so on. His report was inconclusive. But Taluy said to me: "In the absence of any proof to the contrary, Mellaart must be considered faultless. I think the girl was a plant, engineered from Ankara. Somebody knew Mellaart was leaving for Izmir and the girl was put on his track. If a girl like that had a treasure at home, is it likely that she would pick up anyone on a train, taking a chance that he might denounce her? She knew she was dealing with an archaeologist."'

That night, as we prepared to leave for Ankara, it was clear that our story, far from being clarified by our confrontation with Mellaart and the others involved in his life, had become more complex. Mellaart's problems were not simply based on the Dorak mystery. They were now aggravated by an antagonistic Press campaign in front of which there bravely fluttered a nationalistic banner, and by the suspicion of complicity in Ankara. After all, it was a Turk, Hüseyin Taluy, who had mentioned the possible existence of an anti-Mellaart force in the Turkish capital; and if this was true, it was but a simple step to imagine how it would use the nation's newspapers to wound the object of its passions. Were the British archaeologists who had warned us off our researches in fact justified? It seemed they still believed they were.

As we left Kanlica that Friday night, the telephone rang. Mellaart, in the middle of pouring drinks, left the study to answer it. He returned five minutes later, white with rage.

'That was the Institute. Someone's just told me not to speak to you. . . . And I thought he was my friend.'

Mellaart's hands were shaking so much that he could not pour his raki.

Chapter 3

Enter the Secret Police

'Jimmie has a nose for a site that almost amounts to genius.'

The speaker was Sir Dennis Allen, His Excellency Her Majesty's Ambassador to Turkey, a diplomat clipped from a long line of quintessential Foreign Office types whose formal uniform of dark suiting camouflages most personal characteristics. The façade is an amalgam of tolerance, courtesy and compromise. The trick, his trick, is to sit and nod. Only in the most secret confines of a private office or in a confidential despatch can real thoughts and penetrating comment be admitted. We were on the nodding end.

'Of course, you will understand,' he went on, 'we cannot get involved on any official level. You will understand ...' The Ambassador was picking his way through his words as though they were made of glass. 'It's up to the Institute, really.'

The British Embassy squats high on a hill above Ankara in the Kavaklidere district, a suburb of spacious villas. Its drive is lined with unpretentious official cars, while their chauffeurs gossip in the shade. Its gardens are crowded with semi-tropical shrubs and in the grounds a swimming pool gives blue shelter from the burning sun on lazy afternoons. To the north-west the city dips and then swoops up towards the citadel, an isolated fortress defended at one time or another by the Galatians, the Romans and the Seljuks. Broad twentieth-century boulevards quarter the town and end abruptly at its boundaries.

From Kavaklidere, Ankara is seen as a Utopian concept conceived by Atatürk, who when snatching Anatolia from the Ottomans parked his new capital in 1923 on a village and its barren fields. There is no urban tide sinking at random into rural sands: the limits are knife-edged. A taxi drives from hooting, swerving traffic straight into Biblical times.

Back at the Embassy, where a visiting Turk might first become acquainted with the meaning of Britain, its waiting-room is papered with magazines like a dentist's outer office gone berserk. And if the Turk happened to be looking for any sign of the 'swinging' London scene he had chanced to read about in his own sensation-seeking Press, he would be lost. On Monday, 18 July, eighty-two journals spelt out Britain's industrial message. It was not restrictive in any way. The *Hotel and Catering Review* and *The Hosiery Times* fought for room with a cover advertisement recommending 'the top marmalade tart with Moorhouses marmalade' and the *Official Guide to Beeston and Stapleford*.

But we, at that moment, were not thinking of marmalade tarts. Mellaart was all we had in mind.

'You must look at this in perspective,' said the Ambassador. 'There's a long history to it. And it's very emotional. Since the last century foreign archaeologists have been coming and going. Look what Schliemann did with Troy. And naturally the Turks get jealous.'

Yes, we said, we understood this. After all, we had now heard it from both sides.

'Nice of you to come,' said the Ambassador. 'Sorry I can't be more help. Do please call again when you've finished. I'd be most interested to know how you get on.'

The British Institute of Archaeology established in Ankara in 1949 is housed in a villa whose equivalent might as easily be found in Nice or Torquay. Shuttered against the dry heat, its rooms and offices were occupied by archaeologists fretting with impatience for government permission to embark on their 'digs'; their Land Rovers silent in the street outside. In the Institute's private living quarters, floors strewn with Turkish rugs, the director, Michael Gough, an expert in Early Christian studies, and his wife offered us drinks rare in Turkey, gin and tonics. Their hospitality was impressive. After all, bearing in mind the pressures of the last few weeks, we were at the centre of hostility. They, in turn, appeared anxious to act correctly; eager, beneath their natural restraint, to discover where we might eventually place the blame for a situation they seemed to regret. The conversation resembled the opening rounds of a boxing match between adversaries who knew each other only by repute. Our exchanges danced round each other.

'We're mainly concerned,' we said, 'to get a permit to photograph in the museum. We'll obviously need pictures of the Çatal Hüyük and Hacilar stuff. Can you fix this?' The strange complex hierarchy of Turko-British archaeology demanded that we obtained agreement to our needs at every level.

'I think so,' said Michael Gough, still visibly frail from a recent operation in London. 'We shall have to arrange a meeting with Mehmet Önder. He's in charge of the Department of Antiquities. I'll see what I can do.'

'Wasn't Jimmie's lecture in Istanbul marvellous?' asked Mary Gough, who had been there that night at the consulate. 'I thought it was so exciting. Such a pity he isn't allowed to dig. And it hasn't been for lack of trying. You don't know what Michael's been through.'

We said we didn't, but we could guess.

'I must give you one word of warning,' said Gough himself. 'Funny things can happen to your tummy out here. You must be very careful of what you eat. If you do get upset, remember to stick to the three white things: raki, rice and yoghourt.'

His next warning was much more to the point. 'I must confess, we've been worried about your coming out to Ankara, and undoing all our good work.'

We assured him that we hoped not to undo anyone's good work. 'But we thought, perhaps, that we might try to separate rumour from fact. After all, with so much at stake, someone should.'

The Goughs agreed. And we left.

'Ring me this afternoon,' said the director, 'after I've had my rest. I might have some news.'

The delegation that arrived at the Department of Antiquities late that afternoon bore the stamp of defeated suppliants seeking peace terms with their conquerors. Besides ourselves, it included Michael Gough, the Institute's secretary Ferdinand La Grange, and Richard Harper, Gough's assistant. We were shown into Mehmet Önder's office and seated around the wall in defensive positions.

In a country where carpets lie around with the frequency elsewhere of autumn leaves, it is obvious that floor covering cannot be used, as it is further west, as a status symbol of authority. In Turkey, bureaucratic power is made manifest by panels of material fixed to the wall behind its executives. The quality and extent of the material improves with the importance of position. Mehmet Önder's was quite elaborate; significant enough, anyway, to induce in our advocates a delicacy of approach that involved the use of a thousand words where a hundred would do. If we had come to borrow a million pounds, it could not have been more ingratiating. Later experience was to show that this approach was peculiarly English. The French and the Germans are much more forthright, striking attitudes towards the Turks which suggest that in the end they all share the same ambition—to uncover in Turkey, for the Turks and themselves, relics of its prehistory. And it is better done, they seem to say, with spades than with words. It is not irrelevant to the English way, that of all the institutes of archaeology, the British alone is situated in Ankara, founded as it was since the establishment of the republic. The rest, even under Turkish government pressure, have chosen to remain in Istanbul, in direct contact with the centre of learning and removed from Turkish bureaucracy. The rest of Europe, instead, leaves its negotiations to the cultural attachés of its embassies, few of which seek favours, cap in hand. The Americans operate on an entirely different level. The fact that they have invested billions of dollars in the Turkish economy to ensure its stability in the face of Soviet rivalry is persuasion enough. In American terms, to ask is to be given.

As it turned out, superficially, Mehmet Önder was kindness itself. Of course we could have permission to photograph in the museum. He would see that a message was sent through.

'Can we have a letter of introduction? Something in black and white would be useful.' That was the sense of the request. Nothing so bold in fact was mentioned.

'It will not be necessary,' said Önder, with a poetic wave of his hands.

We left, not entirely satisfied that all was now plain sailing. We were, after all, about to work in the museum which had managed to frustrate the ambitions of the Turkish archaeologist in Istanbul, and time was pressing.

As La Grange dropped us at the hotel, he launched into his last attempt to redirect our investigation towards the Institute's viewpoint.

'My dears,' he concluded, 'it is all so tricky. I know you won't take offence, but you don't understand the Turkish mind. . . .'

But we did. It seemed to us not to be so very different from the bureaucratic attitudes of other nationalities. All officials, when they choose, hide behind verbal smokescreens.

At the hotel desk, a message was waiting for us. Arlette Mellaart had called from Istanbul. Would we ring back? She had just had a letter, she explained later that night, from Seton Lloyd asking them on no account to speak to the French television team. As Seton Lloyd himself was expected in Ankara any minute, and the Mellaarts had already been seen by the French, the demand seemed superfluous. Mellaart's comment was brief and characteristic.

Tuesday, 19 July, 4 p.m. The British Institute of Archaeology. Interview with Charles Burney, a lecturer at Manchester University, waiting in Ankara for Seton Lloyd to arrive and for permission to carry on to the Lake Van district in Eastern Turkey, where the two of them, with others, were digging for traces of the Urartian civilisation, a culture that had flourished there around 800 B.C. Burney himself the previous year, their first season, had run into trouble with the authorities. Turkish security had delayed his own personal permit while they screened him, and he was particularly sensitive about his own position.

'For years I was a close friend of Jimmie's, and for years I've tried to damp down the personalities in England. There was wrong on both sides. But with the Toronto letter he went too far. I find it hard to forgive him for that. . . .

'He is unbelievably tactless. . . . What he's got practically adds up to a death wish. . . .

'He's never had to face up to life as 99.9 per cent of the population has. His Turkish wife has been a great help. He has lived in their house on the Bosphorus. He's never had to come into contact with the realities. It would have been better for him if he had had to live in England all his life. It has left him time to devote everything to archaeology, and he has become single-minded to a fault. . . .

'His father-in-law, Kadri Bey, still lives with a kind of Ottoman intrigue. His own investigations into the Dorak business might have helped Jimmie in the short term, but it hasn't in the long run. . . .

'It's a pity, when his case came up . . .'

'What case?'

'Oh, didn't you know? He was going to be prosecuted. The Turks weren't satisfied with his explanation about Dorak.'

'Did it get to court?'

'No. There was an amnesty for foreigners and the case was dropped. It's a pity they didn't go on with it. We might at least have got to the truth then.'

'If that's so, there must be a file somewhere with all the evidence. Do you know where it is?'

'No, I wasn't here at the time. But the Department of Antiquities might.'

6 p.m. The Turkish Foreign Office. To see Zeki Küneralp, head of the Turkish Foreign Office civil service, to check on a conversation between him and Mellaart when Küneralp was ambassador in London in 1964. Sweeping staircases, marble corridors with red carpets, chandeliers, groups of elderly messengers in baggy suits, armed guards at key doors, busts of Atatürk at almost every corner. Küneralp's office was panelled in dark wood, with a large desk, elegant cabinets, easy chairs, and pools of light which emphasised its size. Apart from Atatürk's portrait on the wall behind the desk, it might have been the remote study of an English country house. There was no panel-symbol of status in sight. The room itself was enough.

Küneralp, a tall, thin, elegant figure in a grey suit crossed the room with the aid of a stick to sink into an armchair. He clasped his hands on the handle of his stick and listened with his head on one side.

'I remember Mr Mellaart came to see me after he had had a letter in the spring of 1964 which refused him permission to dig at Çatal Hüyük that summer.'

Had he asked the archaeologist, 'Who's your enemy in Ankara? Find him and you'll know the reason'?

'If Mr Mellaart says that, I must have done.'

'Do you know anything about the court case?'

'There was one, wasn't there? No.'

'If there is no evidence of his guilt one way or another, why should he be cut off from his life's work?'

Küneralp's shrug was barely visible. 'There is a delicate balance between proof and suspicion. He has been made a victim, it is true. But possibly he has provoked himself to be a victim.'

Was there anything he could do, we asked, to help us locate the Mellaart file?

'I am sorry, I have only been here ten days myself. I am sure you will understand, it would be impertinent of me to intervene in any way with my colleagues.'

This was only our second encounter with Turkish bureaucracy, but it was already apparent that to cross the frontiers of one department to the next was the equivalent of leaping from iceberg to iceberg: to put the wrong foot forward was to invite professional death.

'But there is no doubt about it,' Küneralp went on, 'it is a tragedy. I find the whole thing distressing. I sincerely hope that one day Mellaart will be rehabilitated.'

The Bulvar Palas Hotel is a handsome building on the Atatürk Boulevard opposite Ankara's government offices. On its pavement terrace, almost an extension of the departments across the road, the Turkish civil servant drinks his coffee, the American serviceman in plain clothes eats kebab and the English diplomat reads *The Times*.

At half past eight that night in the hotel lounge we met

the French television team, Jean Vidal and René Dazy, for drinks. They, too, had finally got permission to photograph in the museum and we had decided to join forces to save time and take advantage of their lights. And although they were only concerned with Mellaart's work at Çatal Hüyük, they were as interested as anyone to discover the reason why it had come to an abrupt halt. We began to bring them up to date with the facts as they were emerging.

First of all, Mellaart had claimed to have discovered the Dorak treasure in 1958 and to have informed the Turkish Department of Antiquities on at least two occasions before publishing his find in England in November, 1959. Secondly, *Milliyet* in May, 1962, had reprinted his article and alleged that he had been seen in Dorak in 1955 or '56. Thirdly, in 1964, as we had discovered at Kanlica, the Department of Antiquities had for the first time refused Mellaart permission to dig 'until the Dorak affair was settled' and that this was the first outward sign that there was any antipathy between them. And lastly, at the beginning of 1966, his Toronto letter had fallen into the hands of the Turks and because of this he had been diplomatically advised not to apply for a permit that summer, although he had been allowed to dig in 1965, not in charge of the team but as part of it.

We ourselves were following two lines. We had to break down Mellaart's story to prove *Milliyet* was either right or wrong. And we had to find out to what extent the Department of Antiquities' actions in denying Mellaart permits were justified; whether they were based largely on Press reports or on fact. Until we discovered the whereabouts of the court case dossier and examined its contents, we believed the truth might stay obscured. To find that file was now our main objective.

The Frenchmen were listening with a fine concentration. So, too, was the Turk behind them. Ostensibly, he was just enjoying an early evening drink with friends, but for the last two minutes he had sat with a glass to his lips without moving. At a second glance it was obvious he was not sharing in the conversation of his companions. The blank look on his face suggested his ears were tuned in elsewhere.

'But, of course,' said Dazy, 'you must . . .'

'Shall we finish our drinks and move on?'

'But,' said Dazy, somewhat surprised, 'we have only just sat down here.'

'Yes, but it might prove more private somewhere else. Don't turn your head too quickly, but take a look at the man behind you. He's a bit too interested in us.'

Dazy and Vidal slowly took in the scene. 'I think you are right,' said Vidal. 'Let's go.'

We crossed the lounge towards the door leading into the foyer, and as we passed the group of Turks their heads were bunched together like an American football scrum. They were speaking in their own language, but two familiar words floated up. We reached the foyer, and then as though we had left something behind, we abandoned the Frenchmen, wheeled quickly back into the lounge and brushed against the Turks just as those two words cropped up again. 'Dorak' and 'Mellaart' sound the same in any language. We told ourselves over dinner that night that we were fairly sane, and although brainwashed by the current flood of American spy thrillers, not too prone to jump to the wrong conclusion even in an exotic atmosphere that was all set for a story of intrigue. But the Turks had been discussing us, and were familiar already with significant details. Were they just happy pick-pockets of other people's conversation? Or was someone in Turkey keeping an eye on our movements? We reserved judgment.

It took five and a half hours of negotiation at the Ankara museum the next morning before we took our first picture. First of all, the director was not to be found in the city; and then he was. His assistant had the key to open the cases, and then she had mislaid it. Yes, they said, responsibility was delegated, but no one was going to move without the director around. Yes, it was very nice to have the permission of the senior executive at the Department of Antiquities, but he was not the director of the museum. By the time we and the French were grouped round the first Çatal Hüyük object, the Mother Goddess seated between two leopards, our whole emotional range, from delicate persuasion to bristling scorn, had been exhausted. But those were just thunder clouds. The storm broke as Vidal begged for more time. We had been promised a day, he said, and robbed of five hours. All we needed was just a few moments more.

'No,' said the museum's director. 'You'll have to come back next week.'

Vidal went red in the face. 'You behave,' he shouted, 'as though the things here are your own personal possessions. You didn't find half of them. Don't you know that things like these belong to the world? The way you talk, you'd think that we were stealing them by taking pictures of them.'

Perhaps La Grange had been right. Perhaps there was a kind of mind that could not immediately be apprehended. Certainly not the kind of mind that gave birth to the next remark.

'That's just like you French,' said the director with a silky knowing laugh. 'You come back next year—and bring your Paris dancing girls with you.'

A lead to the Mellaart dossier was first of all to be found at the Department of Antiquities. Dealing as it did with scores of foreign archaeologists each year, its first and natural duty would have been to keep files on all. A spiral staircase in the Air France building led up to this section of the Ministry of Education. Our appointment was with Hikmet Gurçay, Önder's assistant. He sat, a heavy figure, in his wardrobe office defended by a large desk. A fan blew pieces of paper on to the floor. Despite the heat, he was dressed courteously in a brown tweed suit.

'The reports in *Milliyet* are nonsense,' said Gurçay. 'We do not think Mellaart has a big organisation to get things out and we don't blame him for all the smuggling that goes on. I can't judge the truth of it.'

Was it the department then, we asked, that instigated the court case against Mellaart?

'We didn't give any evidence to the court, we just told them of the possibility.'

Even so, we said, do you have a file on Mellaart?

'We sent it to the Ministry of Justice. They asked for it when they were investigating Mellaart's last commissar at Çatal Hüyük.'

'Well, if you think *Milliyet* writes nonsense and you have no evidence on Dorak, why did Mellaart not get a permit in 1964?'

'That year he made an individual application instead of through an institute. This is not permissible.' (This was untrue. Mellaart's application had gone through the usual channels.) 'Anyway, we were not satisfied about the Dorak business, because even though the address existed, Anna Papastrati didn't. And why was he so slow in reporting to us? The first time we noticed it was in the English magazine.'

Had he not seen in the file he had passed to the Ministry of Justice, Mellaart's letter of notification of April, 1959? He left the question unanswered.

'I'm sorry,' he said as we left, 'that I cannot be of more help. Perhaps our lawyers can.' His hands were shaking.

If dealing with the Department of Antiquities was trudging through deep snow, our first encounter with the Ministry of Justice was like ski-ing. Melih Ezgü, assistant to the Director General of Public Prosecutions, presided over a labyrinth of dossiers containing Ankara's legal past. He

worked behind one of a series of identical doors and overlooked, and seemed to enjoy, a green garden. Sensing an
urgency in our request, he interrupted a conference.

'We will have no general file on Mr Mellaart,' he said, 'but
we might have a file on his case if it was held here. Otherwise, it will be in the town where the action was brought.
Can you wait while someone goes to look for it?' He sent for
a messenger, who returned some time later with a file containing a single sheet of paper.

'Ah, yes,' he said, peering over his glasses, 'we did borrow
Mellaart's file, but it was returned to the Department of
Antiquities some time ago. The other dossier you are looking
for is in Bursa—that's the administrative centre for Dorak.
You will have to ask the local governor for it. But now the
case is closed, why should we keep it from you?'

The man who followed us that night might just as well
have had a brass band with him. Whether or not it is a func-
tion of Turkish intelligence to teach its agents to eavesdrop
through the bottom of a glass of coca-cola, it is a habit which
is quickly identified. As we talked in the lounge of the Bulvar
Palas to La Grange, assessing the interplay of personalities,
a man who looked like King Farouk sat transfixed through
a slice of lemon, much as his compatriot had done two nights
earlier. Once again we left the hotel with some speed and
turned on the pavement to watch him through the windows
of the terrace. He was scribbling notes. In case he missed us,
we stood on the boulevard until he appeared, and as we
strolled towards the centre of town he shadowed us as incon-
spicuously as a rhinoceros. At the first roundabout we split
and last saw him wondering which of us he should tail.

He was a patient man. Next morning, when he turned up
on the terrace where we were discussing future plans with an
interpreter, he was forced to change tables four times to keep
in earshot as we complained first that these chairs were in the
sun, then in the shade, then too near the traffic. Finally, as he

paid his bill, we checked him with the hall porter through the glass door.

'Yes, I know him,' he said, enjoying his huge Turkish joke, 'he's the Third Secretary in the Foreign Office protocol department. It's a pity he doesn't know how to behave.'

'Oh yes,' said Hikmet Gurçay, on our second visit to the Department of Antiquities, 'we *might* have the general file on Mellaart.' And it was produced as though our first visit had never taken place. The dossier was filled with what Gurçay had previously called 'nonsense'. *Milliyet* cuttings swamped a modest sheaf of official letters of no real consequence. The court case dossier was what we had to find.

That night we sent a telegram to the Turkish archaeologist, Professor Tahsin Özgüç, who was excavating a Hittite site at Kültepe, a village 150 miles south-east of Ankara. Özgüç had been a member of a party of archaeologists at the British Institute just before the Christmas of 1958, when Mellaart announced his Dorak find to his chief, Seton Lloyd. The professor telephoned the next morning and recalled the hectic days of Mellaart's news.

'It was clearly my impression,' he said, 'that Mellaart informed the department sometime during those days.'

Before Mellaart's letter to it in April, 1959?

'Oh yes, I'm sure. It was either by phone or by letter.'

But there was no record of an earlier letter, we said.

'In that case, it *was* by phone. Or perhaps he had mentioned it in conversation to someone. Anyway, I feel they knew.'

'Mellaart has said that he consulted you on the legal aspects of publishing an account of a collection in private hands in Turkey. Is that right?'

'Oh yes,' said Özgüç, 'I remember I looked up the antiquities laws and found there was nothing against it.'

It was clear then, despite what officials might seem to

imply, that from December, 1958, onwards, Mellaart was hardly handling the find with the secrecy he might have employed had he wished to keep the news from the Turkish government. He had talked about it to Özgüç, who, in other circumstances, might have felt compelled to pass the information on to the Department of Antiquities. He did not do so because he thought they knew.

Our last call in Ankara was a return trip to the British Institute where Professor Seton Lloyd was now staying. He had flown in the night before, having grown impatient in London waiting for Turkish permission to lead the Lake Van expedition. He was obviously tired from his journey, but a little exhilarated at being closer at last to his 'dig'. He looked younger. He sat in the Goughs' drawing-room, cutting less of an Establishment figure than usual as he lounged back in a chair, wearing light flannel trousers and an open-necked shirt. He sipped Nescafé.

From the beginning of the interview, it was obvious that he was none too certain of the relevant dates at the time of Mellaart's disclosure. We had checked and cross-checked the sequence of events, and on occasion had to correct the professor. No man, of course, could recall exactly what had happened eight years earlier, but as Seton Lloyd's own version of the story was based on what he believed to be the truth, it was necessary to remind him of the facts. But on the mood of the Institute at the time and on the personalities involved, he was emphatic.

'Jimmie's first account of the Dorak stuff was extraordinary,' said Seton Lloyd. 'I knew there was something going on. There was another friend of his staying here then ... David Stronach ... you'll find him at the British School of Persian Studies in Teheran, he runs it ... Jimmie told me he had something important to explain, but for several days the two of them acted like excited kids, scribbling away on bits of paper making sketches. And then he came and told me what had happened.

'Now, this is most interesting. He said he had come across it six years before in private hands and that he hadn't spoken about it because he had given his word not to until he had permission. And he'd just got that, he said. I thought it was very odd. I found out later that was a lie. He then confessed he did it because he didn't want Arlette to know that he had been staying with a girl in Izmir. They hadn't been married long. The man was a fool not to tell me the truth at first.'

What was Seton Lloyd's reaction to the news?

'I told him, "This is dynamite. You must report this at once to the Department of Antiquities".'

'Did he?'

'I imagined so,' replied the professor. 'I don't think I checked. We were very busy then. All he had were little bits of paper covered with sketches of the Dorak objects. He'd used scraps of our notepaper. I remember seeing the Institute heading on some of them. My wife, she's a bit of an artist, and another friend's wife spent days helping Jimmie to re-draw them.'

Mellaart, according to his own account, had found all the Dorak ironwork rotten, the silver corroded, and most of the grave goods broken by time or ritual. It was traditional in many ancient cultures to snap swords and daggers in half before they were buried with their owners. Mellaart's job that Christmas was to reconstruct the objects on paper in their original and complete form. His two female assistants were employed to help him colour the sketches schematically to show what materials the treasure had been made of.

'Anyway,' Seton Lloyd went on, 'I finally took the drawings to London the next spring and showed them to a colleague in the British Museum and to one or two other archaeologists as well. They were all very excited. But we decided we couldn't very well publish them in a professional journal. Not without photographs as definite proof. In the end, the *Illustrated London News* agreed to use them.'

It was a move that had dramatic consequences. Although the magazine article made it clear that the hoard had been imaginatively reconstituted, it is doubtful whether Turkish officials took the point in. What they saw published looked like a minor 'Tutankhamen'. And it had slipped through their hands. So they thought.

'When I went to Ankara in the spring of 1960,' said Seton Lloyd, 'they were in a terrible state. They hadn't been able to find the address or the girl. I was called to the Department and I told them, "If you don't believe the place exists, you have my permission to take policemen to the Institute, collect Mellaart and make him go to Izmir with you.' But somehow that didn't happen.

'Eventually, a few weeks later, I told Jimmie and Arlette to take the Institute Land Rover and go to Dorak to see if they could find the tombs themselves. And that's what they did. I don't think they actually found anything. I believe the car broke down, but they were able to look down the hillside to the lake and see where the tombs might have been. Anyway, they came back satisfied.'

Seton Lloyd took a long drink at his coffee. 'There's one other curious thing. Some time after all this, my wife asked Jimmie if she could see his original sketches again. There was something she was not too happy about and she wanted to check. Do you know what he said? He said he'd thrown them all away.'

If this fact were true, we later decided, it was damning. What archaeologist, claiming to have discovered rare evidence of a little known civilisation and not possessing any photographs of it, would destroy the only clues he had? A guilty one seemed the first answer.

But then what kind of a world were we investigating any-

way? Events in Ankara had uncovered on all sides deep
emotional stresses. Chauvinism, jealousy and envy were not,
apparently, rare commodities in archaeology, where in the
end a man's prestige depended on what he dug up or on his
intellectual synthesis of the discoveries of others. After all,
one of the most modest and mildest men we had met in the
city had surprised us with his description of the discipline.

'I don't know another profession like archaeology,' he had
said. 'It's so overcrowded. The thing to remember is that on
your way up to the more important jobs, you kick the man on
the ladder next to you.'

Listening to other men's versions of the Dorak discovery
and of Mellaart's work at Çatal Hüyük and Hacilar had its
relevance. But that was like walking round a prism and
catching glimpses of a dozen different distorted views. What
was needed now was direct contact with the evidence. There
was the police dossier at Mustafakemalpasha, whose existence
the Ministry of Justice had revealed. And there were the men
with whom Mellaart had had contact while he worked. Some
of those, perhaps, would be found near Çatal Hüyük. And
that, the Neolithic 'cradle', lay 140 miles to the south.

Chapter 4

The First Sign of Smugglers

Marching armies of the past three thousand years have converged on Konya in slow rolling waves of successive invasions. Hittites, Phrygians, Persians, Greeks, Romans, Seljuks, Ottomans and finally the desperate battalions of Atatürk hacking a twentieth-century republic out of a feudal system; all flew their flags over this Anatolian grand junction where six roads meet. An oasis in a scorched upland, Konya was always a key fortress, guarding one gate to the Taurus Mountains, and surveying the vast plain to the north and east like the touchline spectator on the edge of an empty playing field for giants. It stood, and stands, on the road to Baghdad. And ruined temples testify to the invaders that passed that way. Konya was always a centre of passionately observed religions. St Paul taught there, and Mevlana, the Muslim mystic, composed tender poems within its walls and inspired its cult of the Whirling Dervishes. You must always face God, he said; and his circling dancers, giddy to the point of ecstasy, spun around to show that God was everywhere. Prayers and the sword went together, and Alexander knew its streets.

Our own arrival across the plateau from Ankara was less remarked upon. We drove in in the afternoon, past the mound of Alaeddin, a monster club sandwich of dead civilisations. Ankara's chic secretaries were a million light years away. Many of the Konya women were dressed in Turkish trousers, and those from the villages around still wore the remnants of a veil. Despite exhortations to surrender to complete emancipation, modest wives, instinctive with centuries of religious practice, turned their heads from men or held between their teeth the edge of a scarf which at least concealed their chins. The sheer nakedness of an open face was an advance reserved, perhaps, for their daughters.

We made at once for the local Tourist Office, a square-set modern building on the corner of a street, opposite the shining green-tiled tower of Mevlana's tomb, and sought help to contact Aydin Dikmen, a Konya collector who had somehow acquired pots and goddesses from Mellaart's digs at Hacilar and Çatal Hüyük. Over tea, the tourist official said he would see what he could do. He believed Dikmen was to be found at night at work in the amusement park at the other end of the town. Anyway, among a population of 130,000, it should not prove too difficult to run down our man.

We checked in that night at the Turistik Saray, where Mellaart had often stayed before excavating at Çatal Hüyük, now only thirty miles to the south. The Turistik Saray is a spartan hotel where a request for a telephone call to Istanbul is likely to produce a hard-boiled egg, and whose headiest entertainment is continuous games of backgammon played by local Turks in a pint-sized lounge. It's not the sort of place where you could miss someone. Jean Vidal and René Dazy, the French television team, were unloading their cameras from a car. Both were grey with dust from the plain where they had been filming Mellaart's Neolithic site. They were not alone. They had asked a scientist from Paris to join them for a drink.

Denise Ferembach had just arrived from the Institut de Paléontologie Humaine to examine the bones of scores of skeletons which Mellaart had unearthed at Çatal Hüyük.

She was only one of a remarkable team of world experts that Mellaart was using to examine the evidence dug from the earth: animal bones were being studied at Harvard, grain in Copenhagen, minerals in London, wood in Istanbul, textiles in Toronto, metal in Vienna. Laboratories at the University of Pennsylvania had carbon 14 dating in hand. The complete spectrum of Neolithic life was under analysis in a dozen different cities. And it was Denise Ferembach's job to build up from the bones a picture of the people who had lived on the plain 8,000 years ago.

But already that tiny shy figure was caught up in the web of misunderstanding that seemed to cling to every aspect of the Mellaart venture. During the winter, a doctor at Çumra, the nearest town to Çatal Hüyük, had been paid to re-assemble the skeletons in preparation for study. He had not been paid enough, he said, when the scientist had gone to collect them that day; and she returned to Konya empty-handed. Telegrams were now flashing round Turkey in an attempt to resolve the arguments. Meanwhile, she sat in a corner of the lounge behind a lemon drink that evening and wondered what she was doing there two thousand miles from Paris.

Early next morning, Sunday, 24 July, Denise Ferembach left again for Çumra to bargain with the doctor. Our journey lay in that direction too. Having lived with the thought of coming face to face with Mellaart's 'cradle of civilisation' for six months, the immediate prospect carried an emotional charge. We set out in the afternoon like parched travellers driving towards the first iced drink at the end of a long hot day.

The car shot straight as a bullet for twenty-five miles on a hard asphalt surface, past several ancient wells surrounded by bleating sheep, until we made a left turn to Çumra. The change was dramatic. A deep irrigation canal ran eastwards for two or three miles, painting a green strip several hundred

The following five
illustrations are the
sketches which Mellaart
said he made of the
Dorak treasure in the
house in Izmir. The notes
on the sketches are his
own

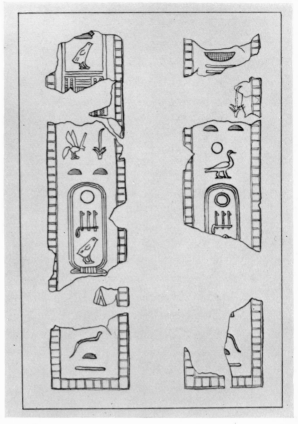

Gold covering for Egyptian wooden throne

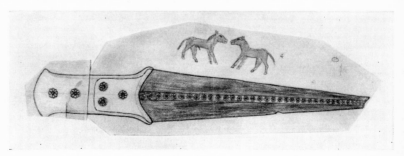

Dagger

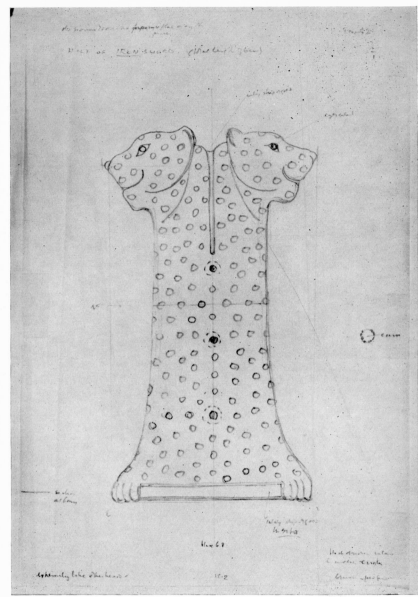

Hilt of iron sword

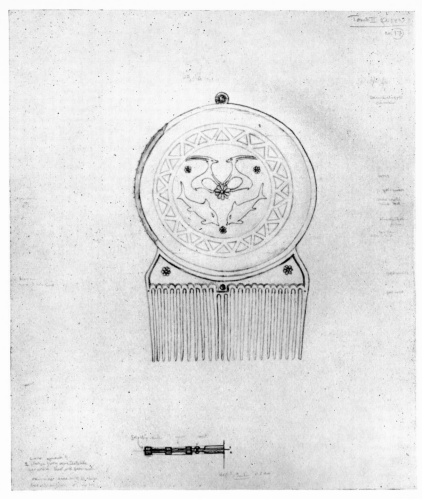

Comb

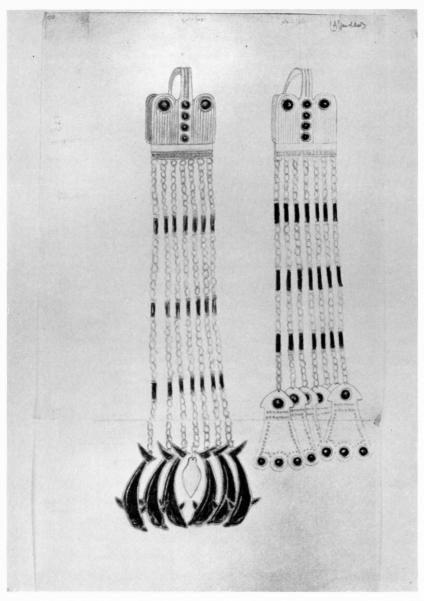

Neck pendant

yards wide across the brown landscape. On both sides of the road the countryside leapt to life to create a broad zone of vegetation not unlike a French provincial scene. Fields of Indian corn and tall wispy waterside trees abruptly altered the scale of the land. The eyes relaxed, no longer narrowed against the glare of a view that ended only on the horizon. Villagers sat in the shade or drove precious cattle along winding lanes. And every quarter of a mile or so chattering groups of giggling naked boys plopped into the canal like startled frogs.

The canal ended at Çumra, a market town whose open central dirt square was occupied by piles of mud bricks and fuel cakes of dung, both drying in the sun; and knots of flat-capped men who argued by the side of the horses and donkeys they had come to sell. On the other side of the town, across the railway tracks, the landscape reverted to type. Empty but not desolate, it opened out, it seemed, to the ends of the earth. It looked like a pancake that had risen in places with bubbles of air. These sudden 'bumps' were what we had come to find. Beneath them were buried the early settlements which had inspired Mellaart on his foot-slogging surveys. We drove past them, not knowing which one was Çatal Hüyük, until we found ourselves in the middle of the village of Küçükköy, whose children at once turned out in force to witness the most exciting event of the day. The women, surprisingly, were none too shy either. They stood by the well filling their pots, while above them perched on the primitive crane which lowered and lifted a goatskin sack, three complacent storks sat on a nest of twigs. Other women crouched by compound walls, working wool on simple spindles. The minaret of a small mosque was the only feature to rise above the flat roofs. Presently, a tall dark-suited man appeared from the most imposing house in the village. It was the *muktah*, the headman, and we were invited in to share his hospitality. The rooms were spotless. Plastic sheets, intensively patterned and highly coloured like some echo of a debased Ottoman design, covered the lower half of the walls. We sat on the mud floor protected by carpets and rows of cushions; and we drank a mixture of yoghourt and water. We had, he explained, overshot the site of Çatal Hüyük. It lay back up the road, about half a mile away. We would find it to the south, beyond a disused well.

Ten minutes later, our car plunged on to a track leading to the tell and we parked. Above us Çatal Hüyük rose like a heavy ground swell to a barbed wire fence that enclosed the perimeter of the excavated area. And as we climbed towards a wooden watchtower, two men strode quickly down the hill to meet us. The first was the official guard whom Mellaart in his Toronto letter had invested with Gestapo qualities. ('He stood right by my shoulder,' Mellaart had said, 'watching me all the time while I dug. It was impossible. If I'd stepped back suddenly at any time I would have knocked him over. And my God, I felt like doing that sometimes.') He wore a grey uniform and a peaked cap with the words 'Çatal Hüyük' inscribed on a badge. The second man carried a gun. He was just keeping an eye out for storks, he said. A note of introduction, given to us by the museum director in Konya, got us on to the site past a notice written in English. It said: 'Keep out'.

The top of the mound was covered with short dry grass and a few fragrant weeds. To the north-west the ground sloped down to a mosquito-infested stream, where corn and sunflowers grew in alluvial deposits much as crops must have grown there when the site was inhabited. From the opposite bank a second mound rose to a height of twenty feet or so. No-one had yet had a chance to put a trowel to it, but its surface was littered with so much Neolithic pottery that it was difficult not to crush it underfoot.

To the south-east, Çatal Hüyük itself ran away to a second and smaller stream, beyond which the plain faded eighty miles towards the horizon. There, a line of extinct volcanoes divided the land from the sky. And in the centre of this black rim stood Hasan Dağ, from which the settlement's inhabitants had brought obsidian for their arrows and their spears. The world was dead silent. A stork, its wings motionless, floated low across the fields and landed, for all its awkward size, with the gentleness of a feather. For a few moments the countryside remained deserted; only slowly moving clouds of dust, like puffs of smoke, in the distance gave any indication that men were on the move. Above, in a glazed blue sky, the sun burned down relentlessly.

In one corner of the tell, the earth had been scraped away through level after level of ruins almost down to virgin soil. There were still two or three levels to go, Mellaart thought, and no one could know what they might contain. That Sunday, chequered with harsh shadows, this excavated temple district lay revealed like a cake from which a huge slice had been removed. All that remained now were the grey-brown mud walls dissolving slowly under the winter rains and snows. Weeds thickly covered the flat floors, and birds and small rodents burrowed deep to nest in the remains. Rough steps, hewn by archaeologists, led the way down to the lower depths. To the uninitiated the scene was dull. All the wall paintings, the pottery, the jewellery and the bones had been taken away for safe keeping. It is sad but inevitable that excavation in a mud town, when all has been dug away to the earth bottom, leaves nothing remaining to tell the passer-by that here once upon a time he had his roots.

To us it was a revelation. If there was little to see, there was much to feel. The tell could not be divorced from its environment or its history. Here, for fifteen centuries, men had shaped a compassionate society in Central Anatolia, which until recently was regarded as a mere barbarous fringe to the Fertile Crescent. From this Crescent culture had been transmitted to Europe, archaeologists thought, through the corridor of Asia Minor. Çatal Hüyük now debates the point: it lays claim to the fact that at that time civilisation was even more advanced in the corridor than in the *grand salon*. From what was now a mud heap, culture had spread into the Balkans and Greece, along the Danube, finally to creep northwards up the Rhine to reach Britain after three thousand years. When it stood thriving in the sun, Çatal Hüyük was four times larger than contemporary Jericho and ten times bigger than the Troy still to be built.

Its list of inventions was astonishing. Here, Mellaart found the world's first mirrors, its first pottery, its first textiles, its first wooden vessels, and its first paintings brushed on to man-made walls. The region provided a peculiar ecological niche in which wild animals grew to immense proportions, and their size was venerated in Çatal's murals. From the distant hills, the ancient tribe supplemented its diet with apples, juniper berries, acorns, pistachio nuts, and they collected hackberries for their wine. They wove animal hair into felt, and made every use of the bones that remained after they had eaten. Ribs were transformed into spoons, knee bones into scoops. They played with knuckle bones in mysterious games, and decorated horns for ritual.

The importance of their religious life was well attested in the area Mellaart had dug, where shrine stood on shrine like a pile of children's bricks. In them, Çatal's inhabitants fashioned the world's first reliefs, each one testifying to a different cult. There was the hunting shrine with its paintings of giant beasts and miniature hunters; the bull shrine with its horns set in the floor and in the walls; the shrine that housed a leopard in relief on which in a succession of re-paintings the spots had been applied each time in a different shape and in a different pattern. And there was the shrine of the Mother Goddess with a relief of a female form possibly giving birth, whose navel had become the centre of an op-art design. The graphic image of at least one religious tradition may have had its genesis at Çatal Hüyük. Mellaart had discovered a second figure of the Mother Goddess, this one seated between two leopards. Was this the Cybele of later classical times?

The worship of woman as the life-giver took many forms: one small cult room was even decorated along a wall with a row of moulded breasts, which, when broken open, were found to have been plastered over the macabre remains of vulture skulls. Death, were they trying to say, exists in the midst of life? At any rate, the people of Çatal Hüyük showed great respect for their dead. Skeletons were buried under the floors of their houses after the bodies had been taken outside the town to be picked clean by vultures in as little as twenty minutes; a practice illustrated on yet another mural where giant birds peck at headless men.

The inhabitants of Çatal Hüyük must command admiration. They were innovators 8,000 years ago as Man has been neither before nor since. They were instrumental in overcoming the barriers between hunting and farming, nomadic and settled life, barbarism and civilisation.

And now all that is left is dust. And the faint sound of the wind across the plain. All we know of them we owe to Mellaart who discovered them. So far he has excavated only one-thirtieth of the site down to the thirteenth level of occupation at about 6,000 B.C. No-one knows what new treasures or revelations lie buried beneath the mound that is surrounded by barbed wire. And knowledge must wait. That is what Zeki Küneralp meant in Ankara when he said of Mellaart's ban, 'It's a tragedy'.

We left Çatal Hüyük that night as the sun slid towards the hills, spreading an amber film across the landscape. The yellow of the sunflowers deepened. A dog's bark carried miles across the plain. The plateau was beginning to spring to life. To the west, tiny dust clouds marked the journey home at the end of the day. The peasants were returning from the fields which had seemed to swallow them up. Some walked, some sat grotesquely astride small donkeys, some packed primitive carts to overflowing. They still live in mud-brick houses. They still paint hands by the front door for good luck. They still enjoy the company of the stork as the people of Çatal Hüyük had done ages before. Little has changed.

Monday was a day of minor victory for one of Konya's visitors at least. At three o'clock in the afternoon, a large lorry drew up outside the front entrance to the Konya museum, and its driver started to unload a collection of cardboard boxes. They contained bones from Çatal Hüyük. Denise Ferembach had struck a bargain: some of the skeletons *now* for what the doctor had already been paid. The rest could come later. She was smiling shyly.

By Monday, too, the Konya Tourist Office had located Aydin Dikmen. Could we pick him up, they said, at the office? He was waiting there when we arrived ten minutes later: a young man of about thirty with a clean shaven face and sleek black hair.

'Would you be good enough to show us your collection? We've heard a lot about it.'

'Of course,' replied Dikmen, 'we will take the car to my flat.'

He lived in the most affluent sector of Konya where the streets were lined with detached villas and blocks of white-plastered apartments. We climbed to his first-floor flat and sat with a drink while he disappeared below. The living-room was furnished at some expense in a style reminiscent of the early thirties. Wooden armed chairs were scattered on a highly decorated carpet, and lamps of convoluted chromium stood on almost every side table. But its main feature was the glass case that divided Dikmen's dining-table from the rest of

the room. It contained at least four rows of exquisite antiquities; only a taste of what was to come.

Dikmen suddenly appeared in the doorway. 'Would you
like to come with me?'

We left the flat and followed him down to the basement.
And there, in a white-washed room about sixteen feet long
and eight feet wide, was his museum. The walls were
covered, almost without interruption, with display cases
which were packed with a dazzling variety of precious
objects: Lydian gold wreaths, vases of Rome and Greece,
boxes of coins. His collection, he said, contained in all about
1,900 items. They were worth at a rough estimate well over
£10,000.

As beautiful as the entire exhibition was, there were several
objects arranged neatly in a corner case which attracted our
immediate attention. It was like homing on a radar beam.
Dikmen had an obsidian mirror from Çatal Hüyük, its unmarred surface in infinitely better condition than that of the
examples preserved in the Ankara museum. He also had
obsidian blades and a necklace. There were other objects
which he claimed came from Çatal Hüyük and were therefore Neolithic, but in fact they were Early Bronze Age artifacts from a site at Can Hasan further to the south. Alongside
these, Dikmen had placed several pots from Hacilar,
Mellaart's other dig.

Hacilar was the second most important piece in the
Mellaart jig-saw. This Stone Age site, 140 miles west of
Konya, had been discovered and excavated some time before
his work at Çatal Hüyük had begun, but in point of time it
succeeded Çatal, producing its most sophisticated pottery
about 5200 B.C. It was as if, when Çatal Hüyük had started
to die, its inhabitants had migrated towards the Aegean Sea.
If they were not the founders of Hacilar, then it was the
construction of a closely related culture.

To the Turkish Press, Hacilar was perhaps even more

closely connected with Mellaart than was Çatal Hüyük. Scarcely a pot of Hacilar could appear in a museum outside Turkey without Mellaart being directly or obliquely blamed. On 15 April, 1963, *Cumhuriyet*, one of Turkey's leading newspapers, had suddenly got worried about Hacilar. Its headline would have brought tears to the eyes of the most hardened dealer. 'Tremendous capital gone out of the country in front of our very eyes,' it said. 'Not even a single object has remained to us of an historic treasure 2,000 years old which has come out of our soil.' Mellaart was the only archaeologist who had dug there, and the implication was obvious. *Cumhuriyet*'s claim, however, would have been quite impressive had it not been 5,000 years out in its date, and overwhelmingly convincing had the reporter bothered to check with the Ankara museum which houses from Hacilar 668 registered items. The fact that Dikmen's collection held some too was of great significance.

'Do you think we could take some of these things out and photograph them?' we asked tentatively.

'Take what you like,' said Dikmen, 'and we'll carry them upstairs.'

We laid them out on a kitchen table and worked our interview towards the vital questions.

'These must have been quite expensive to buy?'

'Oh, the pot cost about £50,' said Dikmen.

'What is your job in Konya?'

'I'm a draughtsman.'

'Is that a well paid job in Turkey?'

'It brings in about £38 a month.'

'You must save quite hard then to buy things like these?'

'No, not really. I do two other jobs as well. Part of the time I do private work as a draughtsman. That's worth about £31 a month. And at night I play the drums in the band at the amusement park. I get about £46 a month for that. It's enough to help buy some of these.'

'Where do you shop for them? With the dealers?'

'No,' said Dikmen, 'that's too expensive. I usually buy directly from the workers and people like that.'

'That's a lovely pot. Where did that come from?'

'Oh that, I got that from Hacilar. From a man called Çetinkaya.'

We took a quick glance at each other. Was this the chauffeur that Mellaart had mentioned in Istanbul, the man who had since become a Turkish millionaire?

'What's his first name? Şevket?'

'No,' said Dikmen, 'it's Ali, Şevket's brother. Ali lives in Hacilar. Şevket's moved to Burdur, you know, the big town at the other end of the lake.'

Burdur and Hacilar seemed the next places we should visit. Mustafakemalpasha and the Mellaart court dossier were getting farther and farther away from us; but they would wait.

We turned to the artifacts from Çatal Hüyük. We had opened up the questioning so obviously now, and since Dikmen appeared not the least embarrassed, the next ploy was the question direct.

'This stuff from Çatal, you bought that from Mellaart?'

'No, of course not,' said Dikmen genuinely surprised by the suggestion. 'I bought them from some of his workers.'

'Is that legal?'

Dikmen shrugged. 'It's only illegal if you take the things out of Turkey.'

'But weren't they robbing Mellaart and the Turkish museums?'

'I suppose so,' he said.

The sad story of Mellaart's last season in 1965 at Çatal Hüyük fell into focus. In Istanbul, Mellaart himself had given details of the bitter way in which the excavation had ended. Two of his servants, planted on him, he alleged, by someone in Ankara, had kept sending back false reports. Even the government inspector, the woman we had met at the Mellaart lecture in the British consulate at Istanbul, had been reduced to tears by their actions. She, the 'agents' said, had been given a necklace by the Mellaarts, and even that, by the time the story had spread abroad, had turned from stone to gold. There was never any gold at Çatal Hüyük, and since the inspector had been given the chore of re-stringing some of Çatal's beads, it was not unlikely that she would have been seen on the site with precious necklaces.

'Weren't you involved in some way with the break-up at the end of that season?' we asked Aydin Dikmen.

'Yes, I was,' he said. 'The government woman asked me to come along to the site that day, and she introduced me to Mellaart's workers.'

'You knew him already?'

'Of course. Konya's not very big and I'd got to know him because I was fascinated with the work he was doing. . . . Anyway, the workmen came up one by one to shake hands. Some of them looked very surprised to see me. Whenever I came face to face with a man I had already met, I gave a little nod. There were four altogether. The foreman and three of his assistants. By the next morning, Mellaart told me later, they had vanished.'

That 1965 season ended abruptly on 16 September in a welter of recriminations. 'The girls were crying at night,' Mellaart said. He sacked the cooks and dismissed the rest of his workers in an explosion of painful disappointment. He could hardly believe that the men, who had greeted him as a friend each summer for twelve years, could in the end betray him. 'I am sick and tired,' Mellaart exclaimed as his faith in them collapsed, 'of being treated like a bandit.' At that moment, the Toronto letter was born.

We left Konya the next day for Burdur and Hacilar convinced of one thing: that even if Mellaart's involvement with the disappearance of the Dorak treasure had still to be disentangled, at least Turkish accusations that he was concerned with smuggling on a larger scale was an allegation yet to be proved. All the evidence so far pointed to the criminal actions of others.

What, we asked ourselves as the car climbed westwards into the barren hills, would the Çetinkaya brothers have to tell?

Chapter 5

The Middle Man
Vanishes

From the south Burdur does not exist. The arid countryside
appears to roll on for ever where only a tortoise may debate
your right to the main road or a single bird pull the sky into
focus. But then the route begins to twist and dip, and each
new turn brings into view more trees, more houses. Unlike
many towns whose architecture grows in scale as one
approaches their centre, the heart of Burdur arrives as a surprise. The way in ends suddenly in its central square, a
glaring open space in a bleached-out town, across which that
day the latest batch of recruits to Turkish national service
wandered out of step towards the army base. The square
contained the usual representative buildings: a museum, an
outdoor café, a bank, two banks, a few shops, the Tourist
Office and a restaurant. A stork sat on a roof at one corner
and watched the idle traffic. Burdur has never featured
prominently in the annals of Turkish history; and looks like
it.

At the Tourist Office, its lone occupant, after attacking us
with German, sent our runners to locate an interpreter, and
suggested lunch next door at the 'Başaran'. There, for the
want of fluent access to the mysteries of its menu, we walked
into the kitchen, as was customary, and pointed to lunch. It
was good and served expertly on the small terrace outside,

where, as we tackled the yoghourt, our interpreter joined us. He was very young, about twenty, a student of Istanbul University at home on leave, and keen to display his excellent English even to the point of saying more than we could have ever meant. It was like listening to the epic monologue of a French film hero when the sub-title is reading, 'No'. Lunch was an open-house affair with inquisitive but incomprehensible visitors presenting themselves at the table to shake hands. Only one man made it clear who he was, and he directed the museum on the other side of the square. Otherwise, we took advantage of our audience to ask where we could find Şevket Çetinkaya. The small committee that met on the kerb to debate this serious subject, we gathered, was prepared to pass on the information to our interpreter. He assured us we would track him down later.

Burdur's main square is well known to Mellaart himself, for only fifteen miles away lies the tiny village of Hacilar, the site which made his name. For four summers, from 1958 to 1961, Mellaart excavated the mound of Hacilar, revealing the first Neolithic site known in Anatolia. He had discovered it in 1956 on one of his regular surveys in Central Turkey, when one morning in Burdur he heard that a local chauffeur had some curiously painted pots for sale. As soon as he saw them, Mellaart asked where they were dug up, bought two, and set off with great speed to Ankara. This chauffeur was Şevket.

The two pots from Hacilar caused a stir in Ankara when Mellaart presented them to the museum. They had no archaeological parallel, and seemed to belong to an unknown culture of a sophistication not previously expected in Anatolia. So in 1958, Mellaart began to excavate the tell. His work uncovered a village which had flourished from 5800 until 5200 B.C., when it was destroyed by fire. The site, however, had begun to be settled at least 1,200 years before. Its community of farmers lived in small houses, each with its own courtyard, and used, as vessels and as cult objects, pots and figurines of skilful manufacture. The pottery was smooth, well fired, and elaborately painted with red zig-zags on a cream ground; the pots were round, oval, diamond-shaped, and even fashioned like a woman, with breasts, arms and delicate faces depicting fine noses and obsidian-flake eyes. Çatal Hüyük may have disgorged artifacts of rare quality, but in Hacilar intrinsically valuable objects were enhanced by sheer beauty. And it had its price.

Their value outside the archaeological world, however, was still unknown as late as 1961 when Mellaart finished his dig. Most of the Hacilar pottery and figures in the world's museums were still under the ground. Those in the British Museum in London, in the Ashmolean in Oxford, and in New York's Metropolitan have come to light since the official excavation team moved out. It was embarrassing for Mellaart, and it seems he could hardly be blamed. He, in his last season, had had to make a choice. He knew he could not excavate another year at Hacilar because, he says, the British Institute in Ankara had decided to switch its line of attack to Byzantine sites, and the money went with it. He could either continue to dig down in the village till he reached rock bottom, or search for the cemetery which he knew must exist close by. Naturally, he chose to finish the work he was doing, so that the settlement dig was complete, rather than break new ground. But the decision had one drastic drawback. Pottery in a settlement site is invariably recovered in a broken state. Mellaart discovered the glories of Hacilar pottery largely from piecing together the fragments of domestic rubbish. But in a cemetery, where it is buried with its owners, pottery usually emerges unscathed. The distinction is important, for unmarred Neolithic pots are at a premium on the world market and, more significantly, in Turkish bazaars. It did not take long for the scavengers, waiting in the modern village for Mellaart to withdraw, to pounce and strip the burial ground. They knew what to expect; they had watched Mellaart's excavators for years.

The road from Burdur to Hacilar runs along the south-east shore of a lake that lies on the parchment landscape like an ink-blot. From the hills it has a shrivelled-up appearance, as if the shrinkage was caused not so much by evaporation as by a slow leak in the valley bottom. Buildings by the lake shore over the centuries were always being left behind. Fifteen miles from Burdur, a bluff of rocks rears up from the earth to mark the village of Hacilar. The cliff is the reason the place exists. It is the reason why Man has not abandoned the spot for 9,000 years, for, from the foot of the rocks, a spring seeps out to dribble down towards the lake. As the water runs, like the canal at Çumra, another colour spreads along its edges.

We parked the car just off the road by the source of the spring, and walked along a track skirting the village orchard. The earth was brittle and pale grey. On the other side of the trees was the modern settlement where in turn Greeks, Romans and Turks had built. But of the Neolithic tell nothing remained. It might have been any patch of ploughed ground except for the occasional piece of broken pot that showed itself above the soil. But further on, like a Great War battlefield, the surface was pock-marked by large craters. They covered the extent of Hacilar's cemetery, and they had been emptied to fill many a museum showcase and a villager's pocket.

We were strolling across the cemetery site, studying the bulldozing techniques of the local thieves, when from behind the trees stepped a stranger. He was dressed in grey trousers, a blue check shirt, and he wore a dark grey flat cap. Neither of us, for obvious reasons, intended to make clear our ultimate intentions. It was enough to behave as ordinary tourists and to document the response. We ignored his presence. He might, after all, have been some sort of a guard attached to the small concrete hut which stood at one corner of the field, its door padlocked shut. But gradually, he drifted nearer to our interpreter and began to talk in low whispers.

'He says do you want to buy anything?'

'Of course. Ask him what he's got to offer and what he's charging for it. But go slowly.'

'You can't do that. It's against the law.'

'Yes, we know that. We're not going to buy anything, but at least we want to know what it's all about.'

The boy and the man talked for a few moments. 'He says he's got something you might be interested in.'

'Has he now? Ask him if we can come to his house and have a look at it.'

He was too clever. 'He says you can't do that, but he will meet you.'

'Where?'

'There's a tree by the road on the other side of the orchard. He'll meet us under that.'

We walked slowly back down the track by the orchard wall to the open fields beyond. There, about two hundred yards away, peasants were sifting corn, and on the right a mushroom-shaped tree cast a jet black shadow across the path. We waited about ten minutes, wondering if we would ever see the man again, when, just as we had decided he had taken fright, a motor bike roared up from the village. It pulled up in the shade. Its driver was a young man in his twenties, in dark trousers and a white open-neck shirt; his pillion passenger was much older, about forty. He wore a dark cap, the crown pulled up from the peak, a multi-coloured check shirt, and over his shoulder he carried an expensive German camera, somehow managing to flaunt it as a symbol of affluence. His fingers were decorated with gold rings. He was about as welcome as the police at a drug party. His first move was to offer us a cigarette, which was refused; and we all then stood around as if each one of us was acknowledging the other's private grief. Suddenly, from the edge of the orchard, the first man re-appeared. He was patently nervous, but not of our visitors. He looked around him and then approached. He was carrying a Turkish shoulder bag made of strips of carpet. Delicately, he removed from it a bundle of cloth and unwrapped his bargain. It was a small 7,500-year-old Neolithic goddess, nine inches long, squatting on her haunches with her arms behind her back. Outside Turkey we could have sold it to any museum in the world for an immense profit.

'How much does he want for it?'

It was ours for £200.

'That's a bit pricey for...' The motor bike's exhaust shattered the air. Its driver tore off in a cloud of dust towards the village, leaving his passenger behind. By this time, like a crowd of leprechauns, ten other villagers had appeared from nowhere. Each was digging into his trouser pocket to pull out a grubby handkerchief. Hacilar's antiquities store was fully open. We were in the market for a handful of Neolithic beads at £40 or an exquisitely carved greenstone chisel head at £70. Trade in the past must have been good. Without exception Hacilar's keepers of antiquities were the most expensively attired peasants Anatolia had ever bred. Gold watches, bracelets and rings glinted in the sun.

The motor bike screamed back. This time the driver was carrying another shoulder bag round his neck. His erstwhile passenger removed it and took out a pot with character-istically pointed shoulders. We could have it, he said, for £160. As we bargained, or appeared to bargain, the motor-cyclist drove back and forth across the boundary of the village keeping guard. Hacilar's police station was just four hundred yards away.

Alas, we said in the end, we could afford to buy none of the objects on offer, but would it be possible to take some photographs? The goddess disappeared back into its sack like lightning. The passenger with the pot was not so highly strung, or at least had a more developed commercial instinct.

'If you do that,' he said, 'you'll take some of its value from it.'

'How do you mean?'

It won't be worth so much, explained our interpreter, if the pictures are shown to other people.

'Surely not. Just one photograph ... ?'

The interpreter and the dealer haggled for a minute or two.

'You can take a picture, he says, for two pounds providing you're quick about it.'

We settled for the price, stuck the pot in the shadow of a hedge, photographed it, shook hands with Hacilar's business section, and drove swiftly off in the direction of Burdur.

It was late afternoon when we arrived back in the town and the streets were crowded with men. Our aim at that point was to make contact with Şevket Çetinkaya, the millionaire middle man who had made his fortune buying from the villagers of Hacilar and selling to the dealers on the coast or to Turkey's private collectors. Our interpreter had heard of him. He was well known in the town, he said, and ran a travel agency in the commercial quarter. We drove straight to it.

'It's over there,' said the interpreter, pointing to a shop by an arcade. 'And they say he owns that block of flats above it. In fact, he owns a lot of flats in Burdur.' He spoke like a man who has just pointed out a criminal in an identification line-up and wished he were elsewhere.

Çetinkaya's agency was called 'Rasgele'. Whether he meant to convey to his clients something of the hazards of foreign travel, or he was boasting of the means by which he had financed the agency, Çetinkaya had a sense of humour. 'Rasgele' means 'By chance'. All the same it was shut. We asked several shopkeepers in the arcade where we could find its owner. They shrugged; they weren't sure. They put their heads together. And then out of the scrum a figure waddled towards us.

'You are looking for Şevket?'

'Yes, do you know where we can find him?'

'I am Ali, his brother. He is away at a garage.'

'Can you take us to him?'

Ali was a caricature of a shifty man. He was fat, with sleek, oily hair, and his eyes never for one moment focused on the person he was talking to. They flickered backwards and forwards up and down the street. He hesitated for several seconds.

'. . . can you drive there? O.K. I will take you to him.'

We crossed the road and climbed into the Chevrolet. The two of us joined the driver in the front. Ali and the interpreter sat in the back. The driver eased out the clutch to slip away from the kerb. Suddenly, the scene fractured like the view in a cracked mirror. The back door was flung open from inside and Ali fell into the street and vanished. A second door opened with a crash and two men in blue shirts hurled themselves into the car, our interpreter sandwiched between them. There was a quick staccato exchange in Turkish and the car began to accelerate away.

'Stop! Where are we supposed to be going?' One of us reached forward and switched the engine off. 'Who the hell are these men?'

The interpreter began to stutter. He had turned the colour of an olive.

'We have to go to the police station. These men are the police. We are under arrest.'

Burdur's police headquarters lay up a hill on the right-hand side of a small street. It was a low flat building, paint peeling off the outside walls, surrounded by trees. Dark and cool. On the pavement its chief inspector, the *başkomisar*, in plain clothes, shirt-sleeves rolled to the elbows, was waiting for us.

Next to him stood the uniformed chief of police, an ample figure that did not quite fit his tunic. Behind them the rest of Burdur's force crowded the open front door. The car was surrounded. We got out, slowly, and confronted the police on the kerb.

The inspector came straight to the point. 'You have been to Hacilar. Have you any antiquities? We would like to look in your car.'

This seemed the moment immediately to clear the air of any suspicions they might be entertaining. We took the two police chiefs round to the driver's door and pulled out from under the seat a handful of fragments of painted pottery, useless to anyone but a serious student of archaeology. The inspector turned them over on the bonnet of the car.

'We picked these up off the ground. They aren't worth anything to anybody.'

He examined them closely and then handed them back.

'Have you anything else?'

We signalled to our driver to open the boot of the car. A policeman began to search in a very cursory manner. He opened one case and looked at a pair of pyjamas with some curiosity. He then glanced under the spare wheel and closed the boot. Had we really been smuggling, we could have got away with the Elgin Marbles.

'Follow me, please,' said the inspector.

We stalked into the station indignantly, feeling secure in our innocence but not at all certain that the language barrier would permit justice to be done. We were led into a small office overlooking the street. It contained a large desk by the window. The two police chiefs sat either side of it. We were shown to seats by the wall. The interpreter tentatively lowered himself on to the edge of a chair in the middle of the room. The rest of the office was filled up with its staff. The Kafka setting was complete. We glared at each other across the room.

'Who are you?'

We produced our foreign press cards as identification. The inspector took them and showed them round. He next directed several quick questions to the interpreter, who turned to us finally and said, 'He wants to know if you would like tea or lemonade?'

'Tea, please.'

The interpreter, who had never been swept into such a situation in his life, began out of sheer nervousness to carry on a private conversation with the police. For all we knew, in his anxiety to acquaint everyone in sight with our virtues, he might equally but unintentionally have been setting us up for a spell in prison. It was time to take charge, very quickly.

'Listen, don't say a word to the inspector without telling us first what he's on about,' we said. 'Have you got that clear? Not one word.' A little firmness on our side was the only thing that would stop him gabbling.

He smiled weakly. 'All right, but I'm only trying to tell him what happened.'

'We appreciate that, but we'll do the telling. O.K.?'

We turned to the inspector who was looking very grave despite his display of hospitality in offering us a drink. 'We've come from England,' we said, 'to report on archaeology in Turkey, and to find out about the smuggling of antiquities. Is it likely we would steal anything and mess up our own story?'

Now he was not so sure of his ground. 'We have to be careful. A lot of foreigners go out to Hacilar and they take things away.' The uniformed chief nodded as if the daily appearance of the world's crooks was the bane of his life.

'We know that, but that's what we're trying to get to the bottom of. After all, you might not know it, but we happen to be on the same side.'

The man in the tight tunic leant across his desk and muttered to his colleague.

'Yes,' said the inspector, 'if that's true, why were you asking for Şevket Çetinkaya?' He was looking over our heads towards the door. There, leaning against the wall, was the director of the museum we had met at lunch. It was clear how the incident had started.

'Isn't he the man to ask for? You should know that. We wanted him, not to buy or sell antiquities, but because we had some very pertinent questions to put to him. Haven't you?'

The inspector frowned. 'What sort of questions?'

'How do you get so rich in Burdur, for instance?'

A roar of laughter filled the room. Our tea glasses were refilled.

'That's a very good question,' said the inspector.

'Is he rich, then?'

'Very.'

'Is it true that he owns several buildings in the town?'

'Oh, yes, he has some flats.'

'Where did he get the money to buy those? It wasn't so long ago that he was just a car-driver.' It seemed very important suddenly to keep the questions going from our end of the office, as both police chiefs were looking slightly disconcerted.

'They say he buys things from Hacilar and other places and sells them for big profits.'

We were muttering to each other to keep it up. 'Why don't you do something about it then? You know, don't you, that English archaeologists are being accused in your own newspapers of smuggling these things out of the country. Why don't you pick *him* up instead of us?'

The uniformed police chief was sliding down deep into his seat. The inspector raised his shoulders in a gesture of despair. 'We've never caught him with anything. And a lot of the time we've had two of our best men trailing him, but...'

We were warming to the attack. 'In that case, go out to

Hacilar and pick up the men who tried to sell us some stuff. We can give you a first-class description of the men. Let's go back there now.'

The uniformed chief wore an expression that suggested that picking up Çetinkaya was his one ambition but that being frustrated in the act was giving him ulcers.

'We can't do that,' he said.

'Why not?'

'Because Hacilar comes under another district. We can't touch it.'

Both officers raised their hands in the air. We had embarrassed them, and so we shifted tactics.

'Well, at least you could see that the place is properly guarded if you're so concerned about the way things disappear.'

'What do you mean?' asked the inspector.

'There's a hut on the edge of the site obviously for a guard, and it's padlocked.'

The two men conferred. 'We can't do anything about that either,' said the inspector eventually. 'It's the job of the Department of Antiquities. It's nothing to do with us.'

'Well, if there was a guard,' we went on, pressing home our advantage, 'where would he come from?'

'From Hacilar,' said the chief in uniform. And for the first time we all laughed.

'Supposing,' said the inspector, having one last shot at regaining his grip on the interrogation, 'we all go down to the town hall. You could talk to some of our officials. They would be very interested in what you say. Would you mind?'

We did mind, actually. We had a very tight schedule, we explained, and had miles to drive before dark. Besides, we told ourselves, there did not seem much point in exchanging the confinement of a police station for the unknown hazards of another Turkish office. Out in the street and a hundred miles away was where we wanted to be. We made a small offer of our own. 'Why not wait to see what we report in England. We shall have lots of pictures then. Perhaps you could do something after that?'

We rose and began to move towards the door, trying not to look as though we were leaving. As it was, they had begun to eye our cameras, and the last thing we wanted to happen now was to lose our films: two shots at least contained pictures of the smugglers. Besides, we still had our own mysteries to solve without taking on the responsibility of helping others to solve theirs.

'All right,' said the inspector with a gold-tooth smile, 'you are free to go.'

We left the police station in a flurry of handshakes and drove to the nearest bar. It was under the trees outside the museum.

Being arrested had not been listed by us as one of the premier experiences to be enjoyed in our trip through Turkey, but yet it had been of great help. Again, it had done nothing to exonerate Mellaart, but it had shown that the smuggling route from Hacilar was a clearly defined example of the way Turkey's antiquities were vanishing abroad. Even the police had Şevket Çetinkaya marked down as a middle man in the chain from the sites, and it was easy now to understand, remembering Çatal Hüyük and Aydin Dikmen, how a foreign archaeologist or even a Turk could work on an excavation, while behind his back valuable artifacts were being fed out to the dealers. Hacilar's cemetery had been uncovered *after* Mellaart had completed his dig, and if the museum in Ankara now housed 668 items from Mellaart's own excavations on the settlement at Hacilar, Turkish press accusations of his smuggling could have been based only on the wildest rumours. They were deplorably short of facts.

Our interpreter was quenching a huge thirst with glass after glass of lemonade, patently relieved beyond all expectation to be sitting out beneath the trees. He had made a few reluctant enquiries when we left the police station of the whereabouts of Ali and Şevket Çetinkaya. They had disappeared, he was informed, and were not likely to reappear until we left town. But, said the interpreter, he had enjoyed the day. Burdur was not Istanbul, and the holidays had been a little tame until we arrived.

'What will you do tonight?' we asked him.

'I shall meet my friends.'

'And what's the most exciting thing you can do in town after that little interlude this afternoon?'

'Get my shoes cleaned,' he said.

At that point it occurred to us that we had done Burdur a small disservice. It *had* once figured in the annals of Turkish history. St Paul had preached by the lake at a time, so it was recorded, when the region was notorious for its bandits. In a manner of speaking it is still.

Chapter 6

The Girl on the Train
to Izmir

Burhan Tezcan is a distinguished Turkish archaeologist who lives in a schizophrenic society, where his countrymen are a Janus symbol facing two ways. In front of them, to the west, beyond Eastern Europe, lies the democracy to which they aspire, advanced technology bringing material benefits to rich and poor, alien cultures which epitomise intellectual ferment, and a sense of curiosity that only the maturer environments can contain without fear of disturbing the balance of the state. To the east, lie their roots, societies built on feudal aristocracies in which order is more important than economic progress, faith more important than belief. Centuries ago, the Turks came out of an ill-endowed landscape to skid to a halt in the face of potential abundance. Since then, like the beggars on the Bosphorus, they have partly lived on hand-outs from their wealthy associates, and they resent it. Tezcan could speak for all of them.

Burhan Tezcan, Director of Excavations in the Department of Antiquities, was born on an archaeological oil field which was first exploited by foreigners, and burnt deep into his consciousness is the one fact that epitomises for the Turks their national sensitivity: it was a German, Schliemann, who discovered Troy and walked off with its gold. Tezcan's xenophobia is as significant a part of him as is his right arm. 'All foreign archaeologists,' he is reported to have once said, 'should be kicked out of the country.' He had also delivered some opinions on Mellaart which were not renowned for their graciousness. Our next step, then, was to find him, question him further on his attitudes, and to uncover any evidence he might have on the part the Turks alleged Mellaart played in the smuggling game. He was to be discovered, Ankara officials had advised, digging his own site in the area of Uşak, a small town ninety miles north-west of Burdur. It was on the road to Izmir, where Mellaart had first seen the Dorak treasure, and on Friday, 29 July, we drove into the town at lunchtime. It had the hot lazy air of a Wild West frontier post, with one broad street that petered out at both ends, and two or three buildings of a size out of all proportion to the rest. They were in fact local government offices for a region administered from Uşak; and it was to one of these that we made our way for precise news of Tezcan's whereabouts. The local branch of the Ministry of Education was most helpful. Yes, said its officers, they knew where the archaeologist was, and on a scrap of paper they drew a sketchy map that climbed into the hills and led into the interior. We set out hopefully.

After three-quarters of an hour, when, where two dirt tracks crossed, we decided we were lost, a caravan of cars appeared over the brow of the hill opposite. It snaked down to the crossing and stopped. We got out and introduced ourselves. Did they know where we could find Burhan Tezcan? Yes, they said, they were looking for him themselves. This was the Governor of Uşak's party and they were on their way to two Lydian tombs which Tezcan had just opened. All we had to do was follow them. There was no alternative. Our idea of an intimate interview with a hostile archaeologist had not included a governor and his staff in attendance, but this wasn't the moment to carp. We joined the caravan. For

twenty minutes it bumped and slid its way across the countryside, cutting at one point over a deserted arterial road as
though it were fording a river, and at another halting by a
whitewashed house with a stork painted over the door to ask
its occupant for more explicit directions. At last, our objective
crept into sight. There on the horizon two symmetrical
hillocks rose from the skyline like the breasts of a woman.
They were not natural; they had been built by the Lydians
about 400 years before the birth of Christ in order to cover
stone tombs for dead princes. The cars, mostly Land Rovers,
began to rear and swerve over the final stretches of the roller-
coaster track to stop at the foot of the nearest tumulus, and
we finished the rest of the journey on foot on a path that
picked its way upwards between the scrub.

At the top, the nipple of the hill had been split open as if
by a giant axe. The cutting led down to the first of the tombs
and in it stood Tezcan, a lean sunburnt figure in scarred
boots, khaki slacks and bush jacket, and sun glasses. A soft
hat with a dented crown sat perched on the back of his head.
He was of course expecting the governor, but we were the
cause of some surprise and a good deal of private conversation. Nevertheless, this was a moment of great pride for him
and he treated us as welcome sightseers. The tomb, naturally,
was empty. It had been robbed, he explained, by local
villagers of its silver ornaments, but these, happily, had been
recovered and the thieves jailed. It was the theft in fact which
had led them to the tomb, and Tezcan's current excavation
was in the nature of a rescue dig to explore the whole site
before the vandals completely ruined it for scientific research.
The evidence of their persistence was dramatic. Through the
roof of the first tomb, only four feet from the giant slab door
which they had missed, the thieves had chipped a hole just
big enough for a thin man to slip in through two feet of rock.
We crouched in the tomb while Tezcan explained its lay-out
and the burial ritual of the Lydians. His mind was not on the

job. It seemed to him that everyone knew what we were doing there except himself, and his courtesies barely covered the sense of unease he felt at our presence. He was not really deceived by the innocent questions we were forced to ask in our role as 'authors on the delights of Turkish archaeology'. Neither was the governor's party which stood a little way off and talked in low voices like the cast of a stage mutiny. Sooner or later we had to get to the point, but in the meantime we prattled away like the vicar's wife making conversation at a very sticky garden party. But then suddenly the governor had completed his inspection. Everyone shook hands with everyone else as if taking part in the finale of an old silent film which a modern projector had speeded up, and we were being swept along with the official party back down the hillside towards the Land Rovers. Subtlety went overboard; there were four hundred yards between us and the end of the interview. The path down was dangerous.

'Watch out for that hole,' said Tezcan in his impeccable English. We all held on to each other like old ladies crossing a main road.

'As Director of Excavations, perhaps you can tell us just how many digs there are going on in Turkey?'

'About seventy,' said Tezcan.

'How many of them are foreign?' we asked, cruising a few feet on a landslide.

'About a third,' he said, slipping sideways into a bush.

'Are you happy having as many foreigners as that digging out here?'

Tezcan stopped and stared at us. 'I don't mind as long as their only purpose is scientific.' The words came out like grapeshot.

'What do you mean by that?'

'They're not scientific, that's all. Some of them, anyway.'

'What do you think of Mellaart?' we asked, hanging on to a small thorn tree.

Tezcan laughed. 'He's not scientific. He never finishes his digs. He helped the smugglers at Hacilar by leaving the cemetery unexcavated. *That's* what I mean by being unscientific.'

'That wasn't his fault. He was given just one more year to dig. He had to leave it. You might blame the British Institute in Ankara, but you can't blame him.'

Tezcan was unconvinced.

We had a hundred yards to go. 'Do you mean to say, then, that you're punishing all English archaeologists for what you think Mellaart's done?'

'Why should we do that?'

'Well, the French and the Germans don't seem to be having any trouble, and Ankara's full of Englishmen sitting around waiting for permits. There's Seton Lloyd and Burney, for instance, spending their digging money on just living in Ankara. Where's their permit?'

Tezcan dug his boots into the scree and turned. 'My department's not the only one that has to approve the permit. It must be passed by the Ministry of Defence and the Ministry of National Security, and then agreed by the whole Cabinet *and* the Prime Minister. It's not my department that's holding them up. Try asking the Ministry of Defence that question.'

Tezcan's implication was obvious: since this Ministry is responsible in Turkey for the security of its frontier regions, and the Seton Lloyd–Burney expedition was bound for its second season at Lake Van, only 100 miles from the Russian border, some new factors were conditioning the Government's decision.

'Why are they involved?' we said.

Tezcan laughed again. 'You ask your friends.'

To ride the road from Uşak to Izmir is to squeeze the study of several sciences into a short car journey. All the way the land is dropping from the summer dry heat of Central Anatolia to the fertile slopes of the Aegean shore where once again trees begin to furnish the world. The route attacks the senses. Into fields of ochre-coloured corn filters the juice green of grapes and cotton plants. Antiquity knew this way to and from the interior and its length is marked with ruined villas, temples, castles and caravanserai. After the dust of the plain, the visual impact of the coast is like a shower. The centuries have rolled on again, and there are lawns, palm trees, boulevards, restaurants, terraces, sand beaches, white hotels, time to sit and stare, and a smooth blue sea to stare at.

Izmir itself is one of the great Mediterranean ports, a natural harbour that eats into the shore in the shape of a bull's head as far as the mud flats that lie under the hill at Bayrakli. Here the city first took root 5,000 years ago. Homer, they say, lived in what was once called Smyrna. The Aeolians, the Lydians and the Ionians fought over it. Alexander the Great rebuilt it. One of the Seven Churches of Anatolia was raised within its boundaries; and blood was spilt there by the Byzantines in the name of God and by the Seljuk Turks in the name of Allah. Izmir was a gate that swung both ways, and trade arrived by boat or by camel. Today, it is a throbbing city of 300,000 people, sprawling along an industrious waterfront, from which ferryboats sail in fifteen minutes across the bay to the district of Karşiyaka. The coast road to the north which heads for Pergamum, cuts through a factory area on the edge of the main town and then skirts the bay, edging between an American sports base and slaughterhouses where the smell of blood fills the air with the reek of iron. After twenty minutes, the road into Karşiyaka itself swings left and then turns again into a narrow high street. On Saturday, 30 July, it was packed with traffic and shoppers: it was easier almost to drive on the pavement. We were searching for Hüseyin Taluy, the former chief of police of Izmir, who had since taken over the police school in Ankara but was now said to be home on holiday. Taluy was the man whom Kadri Cenani, Mellaart's father-in-law, had asked to undertake a private investigation in the summer of 1964, soon after the Department of Antiquities had indicated by letter that Mellaart was not to be given a permit to dig at Çatal Hüyük until the Dorak affair had been settled. The investigation was to try to locate the mysterious Anna Papastrati at the address from which she had written: 217 Kazim Dirik street, Izmir. The Department of Antiquities in an earlier search for the address had been unsuccessful: they had been examining the town back across the bay where the only Kazim Dirik street was an avenue of commercial buildings.

We ran Taluy's apartment to ground in 1373 street just off the shopping centre, about three hundred yards from the sea. It lay on the third floor of a small block, at the top of a bare, echoing marble staircase. A small dark woman answered our ring and showed us into a hall where we waited while they finished lunch. After ten minutes we were ushered into the sitting-room which on its south side had large glass doors opening on to a terrace. The view across the bay was superb. The room itself was decorated in typically Mediterranean middle-class taste, much as Aydin Dikmen's flat had been in Konya. There was a fair spread of mahogany veneer furniture, glass and brass; and small tables were crowded with photographs, ashtrays and ornaments.

Hüseyin Taluy rose to greet us. He was tall for a Turk, nearly six feet, and plumpish. His hairline was receding, and clearly he was about as off-duty as he could be, wearing an open-neck shirt, grey flannels, a green cardigan and a pair of slippers. As with all our interviews with Turks, our questions were preceded by the drinking ceremony which it would have been impolite to refuse; and a little girl of three or four handed round coffee in brightly gold-patterned cups which were specially removed from a glass cabinet. Over the coffee

The Bedestan section of the Covered Bazaar in Istanbul. Here, genuine and faked antiquities are on sale at most stalls. They include material from the cemetery site at Hacilar

A dealer in the Covered Bazaar in Istanbul offers a Hacilar goddess for 300 dollars. It was, he said later, a fake and worth only 30 dollars

we explained to Taluy the reason for our visit. The explanation was none too direct: it was buried in a mass of small talk as Turkish custom dictates. As a race the Turks appear to be easily offended by frontal assaults, preferring the oblique approach in discussion. It is as though in order to get to the aircraft carriers of their conversational fleets, one must circumvent, or pay homage to, the minesweepers, the frigates and the destroyers of their escort. But eventually, the nub must be reached.

'Is it true that Kadri Cenani came to Izmir in 1964 and asked you to help him look for Anna Papastrati?'

'Yes,' replied Taluy, 'as I remember that's what happened.'

'And you put your best man on to it?'

'Yes.'

'That was Yïlmez Çapin?'

'Yes,' said Taluy, 'he was the man responsible at that time for all investigations into smuggling and drug-trafficking.'

'Can you remember what conclusions you came to at the end of the inquiries?'

'I . . . think so. It was a long time ago . . . but if Mellaart had not been faultless, we would have arrested him. You can be sure of that.'

'You think he is innocent?'

'Well,' he said, 'nothing's been proved against him.'

'In that case, if Mellaart was not to blame, was his meeting with Anna Papastrati on the train a coincidence?'

'No, I think she deliberately picked him up.'

'What makes you think that?'

'Because the girl wouldn't have revealed what she knew to a stranger for fear of being denounced. She must have known that Mellaart was an archaeologist. She must have been a plant.'

'But who would have planted her there?'

'Ah,' said Taluy, 'that's the key to the problem.'

'Could it perhaps have been someone in Ankara jealous of his success?'

Hüseyin Taluy smiled slowly, inclining his head on one side. At the same time his shoulders rose in an eloquent knowing shrug. But whether he acknowledged the possibility or accepted the probability, the gesture hovered in no-man's-land.

We had lunched at the Tillâ restaurant on the Karşiyaka waterfront, along which, under the palm trees, a line of unemployed taxis queued in the shade. We asked the driver at the head of the line if he had ever heard of a Kazim Dirik street in Karşiyaka. To our surprise he said he had.

'But it's not called that any more. It's 1777 street you want to ask for. They change the names around here so often that it's only us taxi-drivers that can keep up.' And he pointed the way to the main road going north and indicated that it lay along that somewhere.

The street called 1777 in fact cut across the main highway at right-angles, and we pulled up at the crossing to debate which way we should turn. We tossed for it and headed right towards the hills. At the top of the road we could see several large villas. Perhaps it was here that Mellaart had stayed. A hundred yards along on the left the narrow lane widened slightly to take in a courtyard shaded by a tree so large that it seemed to embrace the community. Its branches formed the roof to a terrace café where several men sat smoking from hookahs, and two musicians with a drum and a pipe made the air throb with a wild hopping rhythm. We called across to the nearest coffee-drinker and asked when was the street last called by its previous name. He took the hookah pipe from his mouth.

'Five years,' he said.

'No, it isn't,' said his friend. 'It must have been ten.'

We left them arguing and returned to the main road. The numbers we had seen on the houses did not even reach 'forty'.

To the south 1777 street sloped gently to the bay. It was cobbled and twisting. It had no identity; it was a mixture of open spaces and close-packed houses which had sprung up spasmodically as the neighbourhood spread slowly from the confines of the waterfront to the cooler luxury of the hills. At once, we were lucky. Two hundred yards down on the right, a small detached house, painted cream, with a red-tile roof, squatted by the roadside. A gate in the wall by the side of the house led to a tree-filled garden. To the right of the door, painted on the wall, was its number: 217.

We knocked on a glass pane of the front door but it was minutes before the garden gate at the side was opened a few inches. We explained to a middle-aged woman that we were interested in her house because a girl we had known had lived there. She led the way through the garden and up some steps into a cool whitewashed hallway. Our interpreter pointed to his shoes and we removed ours as seemed to be required in this suburban household where carpets were more numerous than chairs. A house of women took us through the coffee ceremony. The widowed daughter, who had led us in, lived with her aged mother and aunt. Both, though in separate rooms, were reclining on large piles of cushions. They had, they said, been living in the house for thirty years, but had never heard of Anna Papastrati.

'How long did this friend of yours live in this street?' asked one of the old women.

'About eight years.'

'Ah, well, the house numbers have been changed lots of times. They've been changed four times in the last twelve years. It can't be this house.'

Karşiyaka's local authorities clearly had a drastic way with expansion. It was obvious why official investigators had not

been able to find the exact address. It was bad enough keeping up with changing streets without the puzzle taking on a
further dimension with changing numbers. And so, somewhat chastened by the news, we recovered our shoes by the
back door and left.

The only clue we now had was Mellaart's description: a
two-storeyed house, close to the road, with a garden at the
side. Nothing resembled this for the next three hundred
yards, until at a slight curve in the road, a house on the right
behind iron gates attracted our attention. It was slightly more
imposing than its neighbours, but it was obviously abandoned
and over-grown and, the postman who was passing told us,
had been that way for twenty years. Further towards the sea,
where the road widened and a section of crowded cafés over-
flowed on to the pavements, the street forked. The way to the
right was labelled '1777'; to the left was '1775'. But which
was the old Kazim Dirik street? We pulled in to a kerbside
table and asked. Our route lay to the left. But in fact at the
corner where the road split stood one more confusing element in this trail of changing identities: another 217. It was a
mosque.

Beyond it, as the street swung down to the bay, there were
open patches of scrubland, but at 195 a large dilapidated
mansion stood in fairly extensive grounds. Its exact lay-out
was not clear from the road as it was hidden behind a high
wall and heavy blank metal gates. We pulled the bell rope,
and then again; and just as we were about to turn away, one
door creaked open. A little woman of about sixty stood
there.

'We're looking for an old friend called Anna Papastrati
who used to live in this house; at least we think she did. She
asked us once if ever we were in Izmir to drop in. Is she still
here?'

She looked us over. 'There's no one here called that now.'
'Has there ever been?'

'I don't know, but you have probably got the wrong address. The number's been changed at least six times while we've lived here—and that's nineteen years.'

'So you've never heard of the girl?'

'Well, as it happens, I have. Some people came and asked for her before.'

'When?'

'A year ago. Or maybe it was two.'

'Do you know who they were? Perhaps we know them as well.'

'They didn't say. Just people,' said the old woman, and she closed the door.

Either Anna Papastrati had been associated with this house; or other investigators had thought, as we did, that the place fitted Mellaart's description. Suddenly, as we stood there staring at the gate, the elusive girl became a reality. To hear her referred to by a third party gave some substance to a figure which had hovered in our imaginations ever since we landed at Istanbul three weeks before. If she ever existed, she seemed now more tangible. Still a wraith, but one with a sharper focus. This, however, was the closest we were to get. By now, Kazim Dirik street was thinning out into larger greener plots. The main railway line to the north cut straight across the road, and beyond it the houses to the sea could not by any standards fit the bill. There remained one last lead to explore. Our interpreter had pointed out that the records of each small district were kept by a local official, and so we tracked down the registrar for this area in his house in a small nearby cul-de-sac. But here, too, we drew a blank. He stood on his doorstep and explained.

'There have been no Papastratis in this district while I have lived here and that is many years.'

'Do you know who owns the big house at 195?'

'Ah, yes,' said the registrar, 'he is the only foreigner in the street. He is Italian.' He then began to chuckle to himself.

'He has a wife,' he said, 'but he also has a girl friend in Izmir. It is well known.'

'Is she Turkish?'

He shrugged. 'I don't know. We've never seen her. We only know she exists.'

'Could we find her, do you think?'

'You could search Izmir.'

With our resources such a search would have been impracticable. It might have taken months and then proved fruitless.

'There's one other thing,' we said. 'We are trying to find out which house was numbered 217 in 1958.'

'Well, my friends, that may be impossible. The numbers change so often, I can't remember. I don't even believe we have official records of them all.'

He was right. When we left Izmir, our interpreter offered to complete the search. He won the co-operation of the Karşiyaka chief of police, but even with his help he came to a dead end. But he uncovered one item of information that could have dropped into the jig-saw. During the Greek occupation a Papastrati family, tobacco dealers, had lived in the commercial quarter of Izmir. It was in these years, around 1922, that the girl had said the collection had been recovered from the graves. All the same, it was frustrating. If what Mellaart had said was true, we had stood in a street once called Kazim Dirik and must have passed within a few yards of where the Dorak treasure had been hidden.

But for the moment, Anna Papastrati had vanished off the face of the earth.

Chapter 7

The Big Dealers

In that winter of 1958 in Ankara, just before Christmas, when the British Institute was filled with archaeologists and their wives, the atmosphere was euphoric. In the house at 28 Tahran street, Mellaart had announced his discovery of the Dorak treasure to his chief, Seton Lloyd, and excitement at the news, for all its esoteric quality to the layman, ran there through everybody's veins. Not one voice was raised to challenge the treasure's authenticity: it all seemed possible. No one, at least out loud, questioned the circumstances in which it had been found. A discovery of this calibre was always likely to come from this region of North-West Turkey, rich archaeologically yet closed to excavators for many years while under the control of the military who guarded the approaches to the Sea of Marmara. The great power of Troy was unlikely to have stood in isolation. It was known that between there and the Hittite capital of Boğazköy, eighty miles east of Ankara, several small kingdoms had existed equal in wealth and affluence, but of which no trace remained. Sooner or later some remnant of their lives had to appear. The material from the village of Dorak that Mellaart had seen was, if his diagnosis was correct, the first important relics of the Yortan people, neighbours of the Trojans, to come to light. Until Mellaart's encounter with the girl on the Izmir train, the only first-hand knowledge archaeologists had of this race was deduced from their pottery; it now looked as

though their metallurgical skill exceeded all expectations. In
fact, at around 2500 B.C., a date contemporary with that of
the Royal Sumerian graves at Ur, their manufacturing techniques were second to none. And the Institute as a whole
thrilled to Mellaart's description of what the gold cups and
bracelets, the silver figurines, and the jewel-encrusted daggers
of the Yortan kingdom must have looked like in their
original state. The wives of two other archaeologists at the
Institute were only too keen to help translate Mellaart's thin
pencil sketches of the Dorak hoard into coloured crayon
drawings which made some attempt to convey the pristine
beauty of the grave goods when they were first buried with
the king and queen on the hillside overlooking Lake
Apolyont. It was no secret either in Ankara that this work
was going on. Professor Tahsin Özgüç, a Turkish colleague
of Mellaart's, was party to the preparation of the Englishman's report, and he would never have been the member of
a clandestine plot to conceal the discovery from the authorities. There was an even stronger reason for believing that the
news had spread abroad. At that time, the Mellaarts enjoyed
the friendship of Ahmed Donmez, a senior official in the
Department of Antiquities. So close a friend was he that
Mellaart often said he thought the Turk would have married
Arlette given half the chance. And in casual conversation the
Dorak treasure had been mentioned to him, and he had
shown no immediate concern. Such was his attitude to the
entire affair that when in the summer of 1960 the treasure
seemed to have disappeared from Izmir, his only comment
was, according to the Mellaarts, 'Never mind. I am glad
that you saw it at least. If it is ever found, we can now prove
that it belongs to Turkey.'

Since then, however, Donmez had vanished from the
archaeological scene to surface eventually in Izmir as the
director of its annual trade fair. No one can quite explain his
change of hats. It seemed strange that in mid-career a promis-

ing archaeologist with his specialist knowledge should suddenly switch to being an organisation man arranging business deals. The two were poles apart. It was as if in Britain the Boat Show had been taken over by an excavator from the Ministry of Works.

In Izmir, Ahmed Donmez's office was on the first floor of a modern block, facing a main boulevard on the edge of the trade fair park with its lakes and coloured fountains. His secretary explained that her boss could only give us a few minutes as this was his busiest day of the year. His outer office was filled with suppliants for display-stand space. They sat, caps and papers in hand, each waiting to impress upon Donmez the supremacy of their demands. There were Libyans, delegates from Central Africa, and Turks who looked as though they had only enough capital to run a cheap souvenir stall in the local bazaar. We waited with them for half an hour until finally we were shown in. Even then we could not lay claim to his undivided attention. Every few moments assistants rushed in with documents for him to sign. Donmez sat behind a large desk with a view over the lush green park. He was short and carefully dressed in a tropical suit. He had a full face which smiled a lot, and his eyes were creased with humour. He came straight to the point and made it clear that we were tackling a dangerous subject and, as far as he was concerned, hitting a nerve end.

'I will talk to you about archaeology in general, and about tourism and the fair,' he said, 'but about this Dorak business, I have nothing to say.'

It was a long way to come to hear that, but we *were* in his office and the only thing to do was persevere. We had to know whether or not Mellaart had informed the Department soon after his discovery, as he claimed, and when the Turks had taken action. The question was: had Mellaart done it immediately or not until his account was published in the *Illustrated London News* more than a year later? The dates were important because the Turkish Press had so often accused Mellaart of withholding information.

'Well, can you tell us one thing?' we asked. 'When did you first know of the Dorak treasure?'

'I'm a very near friend of the Mellaarts. I've known Arlette for years, so naturally I was aware of what was going on. Did they tell you in Ankara I was slack in my duties?'

'No, no . . . of course not. But can you recall when he notified you officially?'

'Not exactly. It was a long time ago.'

'Did you begin to investigate when you had Mellaart's first official mention of it in a letter he sent to the Department in April, 1959, or later that year when his English magazine report reached Ankara the following Christmas?'

'Well, our official searches began in January, 1960. But I can assure you that I wasn't slack in my enquiries. Have they suggested at the Department that I was?'

'Did you ever say to Mellaart that you were glad he may have seen it, so that if one day it was recovered, you could show it was found in Turkey?'

Donmez hesitated. '. . . Maybe I did, but the affairs of the Department are no longer my business. All I can say it that I investigated the matter as well as I could. I hope that no one had told you otherwise . . . I'm so sorry that I cannot be more help. If you asked me any other questions on archaeology, I could probably answer you.'

Despite Ahmed Donmez's warm reassuring smile, his anxiety lay about an inch beneath the surface. The whole Dorak affair had not only had its repercussions in the hothouse atmosphere of the British Institute and between Briton and Turk, but also in the Byzantine apprehensions of the Department of Antiquities. There, someone had had to carry the burden of departmental responsibility for the apparent loss. Who?

.   .   .

Almost without exception, Turkey has prohibited the export of its antiquities. Smuggling is thus the answer of private enterprise. But this nation's problems are only one element of an international phenomenon. The spread of higher education and its attendant heightening of artistic appreciation has, in the West particularly, increased the appetite for new visual experiences, whether the objects concerned were made yesterday or 5,000 years ago. It may be a Chippendale chair, a Van Gogh canvas, a Ming vase, or a Greek urn, but somewhere there will be a gallery or a museum anxious to acquire it in order to stay in the race for prestige and satisfy its growing culture-hungry public. This competitive aspect of a flourishing market is epitomised, for example, in the attitude of even as august an institution as the British Museum; for its director, Sir Frank Francis, once pointed out that if he had not bought a Neolithic pot which had been dug up at Hacilar, 'it would only go to the Louvre or the Metropolitan in New York. And before I knew where I was, I would be blamed for being dull and unenterprising.'

There is, however, another sector of public demand which encourages even more the antics of the smugglers. This is to be found in that area of society where new wealth has created a desire for status symbols beyond the dish-washer and the second car. In a mass-producing world, the greater the availability of consumer goods, so is the demand for the unique enlarged. But only so many Rembrandts, so many Fabergé watches, so many Roman friezes exist; and inflation of price must result to the joy of smugglers and forgers alike, for even if the supply is not there, the demand must be fulfilled. Faking is, in fact, archaeology's latest peripheral skill. East of the Mediterranean, in attics, village huts, behind bazaars, the Van Meegerens of ancient artifacts fire pots, chip marble and smelt metal to supply the insatiable international dealers. And once out of the manufacturers' hands, these objects are rarely put to scientific test. Only the accumulated judgment of dealers, auctioneers and purchasers can give them their pedigree, and sometimes these authorities are mistaken. But whether the purchasers are public museums or private collectors, whether the artifacts are genuine or fake, demand and supply will collide with the greatest impact in that area where the cultural heritage is greatest. The exploitation of Turkey in this respect has, since Schliemann's rape of Troy in the 1870s, become so well-established that illicit dealing is now carried on in the striped-trousered atmosphere of routine business negotiations.

In this aspect of our investigations, so far we had traced the smugglers' passage of Neolithic pottery from Hacilar to Burdur, and we had seen the artifacts on sale in Istanbul's Covered Bazaar, where we were told of an export route through Izmir. But we were still ignorant of the last link in the conveyor belt. And for this we turned to our interpreter.

Of the many men in Turkey who had translated for us, our assistant in Izmir was to prove the greatest contributor to the story. The rest, while realising the significance of our enquiries, played only a passive role as intermediaries. Our Izmir interpreter had more to offer. He had a profound background knowledge of archaeology in general, and a fair acquaintance with this particular line of research. And, what was more important, he had revealed at our first meeting an intimate awareness of underground Izmir. There was little about the alley life of the city that he did not know. But he cannot be more closely identified than this brief description of him permits. He asked to remain anonymous for fear of violence. We shall call him Mehmet.

We already knew from the dealer's invitation in Istanbul that any illegal goods we cared to buy could be happily shipped out through the American Army Post Office, an unpretentious building near the centre of Izmir, accessible equally to American personnel and Turkish porters. It would be difficult to apportion the responsibility for accepting illicit parcels to either, but on observation it was clear that it would be simple to slip a package into the mainstream of mail without it ever having to pass through official hands. And the fact that Izmir harboured a NATO base helped to diffuse the exact limits of Turkish dominion. Moreover, the Post Office was not the only gateway to the world market.

'The airport at Çiğli,' said Mehmet, 'is equally good for getting things out of the country.'

We asked him where it was.

'It's an airfield about seven miles north of the city. The Government calls it "a field with American installations". But the Opposition flatly describes it as "an American base". Either way, it's in continual use for United States jet charter flights. You can imagine, there's little customs control with all those tourist dollars coming in.'

'How do you know all this?' we asked him.

'I used to work there,' he replied. 'And let me tell you something else, you should see what's in some of those American houses. My job used to take me into them. There are antiquities all over the place. Whether they're faked or not, I wouldn't know, but I bet they're all going home with them to the States.'

This was all very well, but as reliable as the information appeared to be, it was still second-hand experience. We wanted, above all, to make contact with the dealers themselves and to prove beyond a shadow of doubt that it was possible to remove any archaeological artifact from Turkey without Mellaart being involved, contrary to what the Turkish newspapers might like to believe. Mehmet, so he said, would arrange this.

Our last afternoon in Izmir took place against a bizarre background of a half-familiar noise. All over the city, radios in homes and cafés were tuned to the local station relaying from London the Final of the World Cup in which England was playing Germany. As a result the Turkish nation was

suffering another of its schizophrenic attacks: it wasn't sure
where its true allegiance lay—with the Germans with whom
it had been allied in the First World War and who had
subsequently invested considerable capital in the country, or
with the English who had once been masters of the game.
There was little joy in it for us in view of the Turkish commentary, except for the occasional roar which at least indicated some aggressive action on the part of the home side.
Our own attempts to make contact with the contest were
neurotic to say the least. Our car radio was turned on
to the programme, but was smartly switched off at our in-
sistence as the Germans scored their last-minute equalising
goal. There was enough suspense around without inviting
more.

Slowly, that afternoon, the car cruised into the Başmane
district of Izmir, where on the main streets and in the court-
yards beyond, the jewellers' shops fight for space. It wasn't
long before Mehmet stopped the car by the kerb where a
small group of men were gathered near a store window, and
he called across to one of them to come over. The stranger
who approached was wearing a loose raincoat over his shoulders. Our companion spoke a few words to him. The Turk
looked up and down the street, plunged his hand into a
copious pocket and thrust a package wrapped in newspaper
through the car window. We undid it. It contained two small
statuettes. The suburban equivalent of the rapacious Turkish
villagers of Hacilar was, so he thought, in business.

'They're either Greek or Roman,' said the interpreter. 'I
wouldn't be sure. They're probably faked anyway.' He
turned to the man on the pavement. 'How much do you
want for them?'

'Forty pounds,' muttered the small-time dealer.

'Too much,' said Mehmet; and without beginning to
haggle, we drove on down the street.

'You see what I mean,' said the interpreter, 'it's as easy as that. And I bet he didn't come by them honestly. But that's only the rubble. Let's see what happens next.'

Mehmet explained that he was going to take us to the shop of an antiquities firm run by three brothers. 'Now take it easy with them,' he warned us. 'They're very tough. If they suspected something, they could get very ugly. I want you to act as though you are tourists. Don't ask too many questions to start with. You'll begin in the front of the shop where they've got a few things. They won't be worth much. But just look as if you're very interested and don't know too much about it. And then see what happens.'

Within two minutes we drew up outside the shop, the front window of which was packed with the usual tourist bric-a-brac. Inside, on the left, was a long serving counter the length of the wall. For the rest, scores of shelves were piled high with rugs and a wide variety of copper utensils. But near to the door, on the right, a separate stack of shelves was lined with antiquities. There was little of distinction: a few Roman heads, some Greek statues and a Yortan pot or two. Two of the brothers stepped forward to greet us. We were introduced and invited to look round at our leisure. Carefully, we examined almost every item in the stack, comparing notes with each other and generally making a few useless comments which Mehmet passed on to the owners. After about five minutes, during which time our friend with great pantomime appeared to be talking us into buying some of the artifacts, we began to look very disappointed and to murmur to each other what a pity it was that there was nothing really old or especially valuable to be bought. There was nothing Neolithic, for instance. What a shame. We had wanted to take something back that was unique. This, we indicated with a wave of the hand, was after all just a lot of old pottery. In our travels through Turkey we had seen some marvellous things. We had to admit that we didn't know what we were really looking for; but it had to be *old*. The two brothers took

Mehmet on one side, and there in another corner of the shop they held a conference. Presently, our companion returned.

'They say,' he said without blinking an eye, 'that if you would like to see some other things, more in your line perhaps, they would like you to follow them.'

We smiled, bowed slightly, and generally, without dancing about all over the shop, indicated our pleasure at the thought.

The brothers began to walk towards the back of the store and we moved after them, disappearing through a red velvet curtain to climb a narrow staircase into a small office on the first floor. The room was sparsely furnished with a desk and four wooden chairs. The floor was bare, but the walls were covered with shelves each of which was crowded with archaeological objects of great value and aesthetic quality. We were in another league. One of the brothers, a short, dark, olive-skinned man with a pencil-line moustache, sat behind the desk and ordered tea. We were in business. He pointed to the shelves. Did the things on them interest us? We made some play of examining them and then shook our heads. He paused for a moment, as though making an assessment, and then bent down to open a drawer in his desk. From it he pulled out a small newspaper parcel which he gently unwrapped to display a perfectly formed squatting Hacilar goddess. There was no need for a moment to play the part of an actor; our delight was genuine. If not a fake, such a figure would have been coveted by every museum in the world. She was a cult object, about seven inches high, and once must have knelt, straight-backed, in a niche in a mud house at the village near Burdur.

We looked the goddess over with extreme care. 'Yes, it's quite good. How much is it going for?'

'Six hundred pounds,' said the second brother from the other side of the room. This was already three times more than had been demanded for a similar object in Hacilar itself. Prices obviously escalated on the coast.

A view of the excavations at Çatal Hüyük. The steps are modern. On the top of the mound stands the watchtower

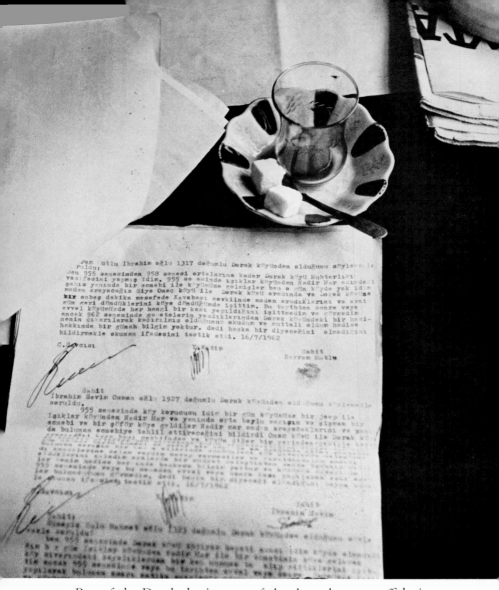

Part of the Dorak dossier: top of the sheet shows an affidavit signed by a villager with a thumbprint. See page 132

We stared at the brothers, playing the poker game as instructed. The brother at the desk stared back. And then slowly, piece by piece, he began to extract from the drawers a collection of antiquities that would have made the focal point of any collection. Some items were screwed up in bits of paper; others were stored in a dilapidated jewel box, wrapped in silver foil or cotton wool. Within ten minutes, the dealer's desk was covered with a jackdaw array of archaeological loot. There were two especially beautiful Yortan vases, an Assyrian seal, another Hacilar goddess—this one standing but broken in half, a Greek urn, a three-neck Yortan pot, a Roman cybele, a Greek silver nose-shield, a Lydian gold laurel wreath, a Byzantine seal, a Lydian silver duck-head vase, a two-faced figure purported to come from Hacilar, several silver dishes of uncertain origin, and a handful of Greek gold dress ornaments—exquisite rosettes which would have once adorned a nobleman's cloak. For the Assyrian seal alone, the brothers were asking £400. At a rough estimate, the total price of the goods on the desk must have worked out at about £12,000.

'Very . . . very interesting,' we said. 'Where do you find this sort of thing?'

The two brothers looked at each other and laughed. The question went unanswered.

The first part of our objective had been achieved. There were the goods on the desk, and we had been offered them in the full knowledge that if we had bought any of them, we should be taking them out of the country. And clearly to do that we should have been breaking the law. The problem now was to probe a little deeper into the identity of the brothers' customers, and finally to extricate ourselves from the premises without upsetting the delicate mood of good-will we had so far engendered. We turned on the innocence.

'These are all very beautiful, but everything's a tiny bit

expensive. We don't carry that much money around with us.'

The brothers smiled and spread out their hands as if to indicate that this was not a unique moment in their lives. They had heard this excuse before.

We pressed on. 'There can't be many people about who can afford this kind of stuff, can there? After all, who *can* carry this sort of money?'

The brother behind the desk grinned broadly. 'Of course not,' he said, 'but then most of our customers are dealers.'

'Oh, from other parts of Turkey?'

'Perhaps,' said the second brother, 'but most of them come here from Europe.'

We attacked their pride. 'Do you mean they come all the way here from France and Germany, for instance?'

The brother on the other side of the room took the bait. 'Further than that,' he replied. 'We get dealers in this shop from England and America.'

'Who, for example?' There was no padding around that question. It was aimed straight at their boast: the chances were they would be provoked into substantiating it, and they were.

'There's a man called Weissmann from London,' said the brother at the desk.

'Do you know his first name?'

'Yes. It's Hugo Weissmann.'

'Do you know him?' asked the second brother sharply.

We had slipped a bit out of our 'tourist' persona. 'Well,' we said, 'not personally, but the name is familiar.' In fact it was not, but five weeks later in London we tracked down Hugo Weissmann and asked him how his name had become associated with the dealers in Izmir. For the moment, however, we were still fishing.

'Do you do much business with America?'

The brothers mentioned another international dealer,

American by birth, who has an antiquities business on the Continent and is a scholar in certain fields of archaeology.

'He is a very tough man. You see this Hacilar goddess,' said the brother behind the desk. 'I will tell you a story. Not so long ago, this man was here in this shop. He was sitting in my brother's chair, just over there. We had been showing him some new things, but he seemed to be dozing off. He had had a big lunch. So we all went downstairs and left him for a while. Some time later my brother came back up here, and there was this man sitting up in the chair and in one hand he held the top half of the goddess and in the other he had the legs. He had snapped it in two. My brother was shocked. He said to him, "What have you done?" And this man replied, "How much were you asking for this? £1,200? I thought it might be a fake so I broke it in half to have a look. But I can see now it isn't. I'll give you £600 for it. It can't be worth all that much now it's broken." My brother nearly wept.'

If the story was true, it showed an astonishing indifference to the beauty of these objects, and argued a mind that was concerned only with the profit motive. If vacuum cleaners had been as valuable, the American dealer might just as well have dealt in them. He and his colleagues operate in that twilight area of legality where, one moment, they commit the act of a crook, while the next deal stands just inside the threshold of the law. They trade in cupidity in a profession whose romantic environment adds a gloss to their manoeuvres which would otherwise be recognised as sordid.

Another thought struck us. If the story was true, breaking that goddess seemed a foolhardy act to commit on these premises.

'You should have stuck a knife in him,' we said, indicating a swift solution to the offence which might also have occurred to the dealers.

'What,' cried the brothers in unison, 'and kill our best customer?'

Fifteen minutes later, and after more tea, we left the shop, content with the results. We had started with an archaeological site near which villagers were illegally selling its artifacts. We had found, if not a middleman, a middleman's brother who seemed after sufficient sidelong glances willing to gratify our request. And now we had traced the smugglers' route to the coast beyond which lay the sea, an open market and enough competitive bidders to send prices to a ceiling whose height was governed only by the wealthiest museum or the pocket of a rapacious millionaire. There were still ends of the trail to be tied up in London and elsewhere, but for the moment we had reached the grand junction. So, grateful for his help, we took Mehmet back to the hotel for a drink. As we sat at a table on the terrace near the swimming-pool of the Büyük Efes, sporadic roars swept up from the bar below. England and Germany were into extra time. It was hard to concentrate. Mehmet was rambling on about the word 'Ana' and its root meaning, a root so long that it must have threaded its way back into the primitive grunts of pre-history; a name at least that Man had used for centuries as an oral symbol by which to identify his Eternal Mother.

'You see,' said Mehmet, 'there's the question of the cybele ... the goddess ... now that word crops up in a dozen different languages. There's ...'

There was a deafening roar from the bar. Two waiters detached themselves from a white-jacketed group by the radio and raced up the stairs to the terrace.

'Effendim ... effendim ... England have won ... four, two.'

It was an expensive night.

Chapter 8

The Dorak Dossier

The dark corridors were crowded with men and women who kept close to the walls as though making an avenue for the passage of a prince. Some wore bandages red with spreading blotches of blood; others waved their arms around in fierce argument; a few stood like statues deep in the contemplation of a minor crime. Plaintiff or defendant, they had come to Bursa's Department of Prosecutions to embark on a long voyage through Turkish law. Like the suppliant figures on a classical frieze, they filled the austere building with images of conflict, violence, pathos and distress. Above them, in a spacious office of workmanlike intent, sat their ultimate hope and nemesis, the director himself, Memduh Oktav, whose face and person expressed the final symbol of justice. Oktav was overwhelming in a paternal way, filling his chair with a mass that inhabited rather than occupied it. His head was that of a Byzantine emperor, exaggerated in every detail; the nose of a Roman, the smooth cork-coloured complexion of a Levantine, the lines were strong and straight, his hair springing back in full grey waves. In a toga, a *kaftan* or a lounge suit, he may never have moved from that seat for two thousand years.

Below wide windows lay his province. The city, sprawling in a gentle fall to the plain, ended abruptly behind him to the south against the ramparts of Turkey's Mount Olympus. On the one main route from the interior to the Sea of

Marmara, Bursa, where two hundred fountains filtered the heat from the sun, had always been a place to covet. Hannibal inspired its origins by recommending its location to the Bythinian king, Prusias, after whom it was named. And once it was captured by Mithradates, only later to become, like so many regions of Asia Minor, a Roman possession, whose rulers valued it as a spa fed by medicinal springs flowing from the foot of the mountain. With its seductive climate of summer and made glorious by winter snows, the alpine city was a battleground for Seljuk Turks and Byzantine armies until both faded from vivid memory under the onslaught of the Ottomans. These invaders from the East made it their first capital and embellished it with monuments. And although finally it ceased to be a city from which they governed, the Ottoman sultans nevertheless returned time and again in state to enjoy its baths and ensure their immortality by erecting mosques and tombs of incomparable beauty. But long before they existed, Bursa boasted of a much more articulate visitor, Pliny the Younger, whom Trajan had despatched from Rome to unravel the provinces' financially entangled affairs. Like modern speculative property developers, Bursa's leading citizens had plunged into a building programme that had left them noble with achievement and saddled with debt. Pliny sat in judgment on these incautious crooks, and now Memduh Oktav wore his robes.

Of course, he offered drinks, and we welcomed the courtesy. It gave us a chance to assess the man whose word would open the Dorak dossier. He had every right to consider that the matter was of concern only to his department. Certainly, a Turkish journalist in England would get short shrift from the authorities faced with a similar request. He leant across his desk.

'Tell me what you want?'

We recited a shortened version of the story, while he

nodded as if at the back of his mind small tumblers in a combination lock were falling into place.

'Yes,' he said at last, 'I know the file you are talking about. But it's not here in Bursa. It will have been kept in my department in Mustafakemalpasha. You know where that is? Good. It's the nearest town to Dorak. It's where the case would have been heard if we had proceeded with it. My assistant there has all the papers.'

'We'd very much like to see them wherever they are. Now that you're finished with them, we thought you wouldn't mind giving us a look. It seems the only way to kill the rumours once and for all.'

Memduh Oktev pressed his broad back into his chair and spread his hands flat on the desk. He stared at his fingers for what seemed like hours. A broad smile grew on his face and slowly he lifted his head.

'Yes,' he said, 'I see what you mean. I think that is reasonable. I will tell them to give you the file.'

If release of tension was a visible emotion, it would have been seen that morning in Oktav's office rising like a cloud of steam. Nevertheless, his word was one thing. It remained to get his authority down on paper.

'Perhaps you would like us to wait in your outer office while you dictate some sort of order. Wouldn't that be the best thing?'

'That will not be necessary,' he said firmly. 'When you leave, I shall telephone to Mustafakemalpasha and tell the local prosecutor to let you see everything you want. You will, I presume, go there at once. I will tell him to expect you at two o'clock. I will telephone him. That will be enough.' The emperor had spoken.

Outside the office, we made plans to leave Bursa immediately. Was this all right with our interpreter? He hesitated a little. Ayhan Utul had been recommended to us by Mehmet in Izmir where they had worked together with tourists, and we had picked him up at the Tourist Office in Bursa on our arrival.

'It may be difficult for me,' he said, 'as you are now involved with another government department. It is a very delicate thing for me to be poking my nose into other sections. I should have to get the permission of the Governor.'

'Right,' we said, determined now not to let any obstacle get in the way. 'We'll go and see the Governor.'

'What, now?' said Utul, who looked as though he would have been a lot happier if the negotiations were to be executed with a little more finesse.

'Yes. Right now.'

If Bursa's Public Prosecutor was paternal in the operations of his office, its Governor was nothing less than avuncular; for no matter how shrewd his brain might be, no matter how incisive his political decisions, he obviously acted behind a façade of unmitigated charm. He rose from his desk to fill the room. His slightly stooping figure was clothed in a brown light-weight suit. His thinning grey hair was brushed back from his forehead, and he shook hands with a mammoth paw.

Ayhan Utul launched into an explanation in a slightly feverish tone of voice. The Governor listened patiently, supporting the rest of his expression on a jutting lower lip.

'My dear friends,' he exclaimed as Utul finished speaking, 'I am delighted that you have this opportunity to carry on with your investigation. And you really need this man? Excellent. Then you shall have him. He can tell his director I have said so. Now, there is one thing. When you open that dossier, I ask you to remember this. The quality of English justice is renowned throughout the world. I trust you will read the papers carefully and come to a right decision. That is all I ask.'

Overcome by Bursa's Portia, it was an appropriate moment to succumb to Byzantine manners; and so, filled to the ears with tea, we made suitable comments about the nation's hospitality. And with terse farewells expressed in the West European form rendered more awkward by the Governor's poetic turn of phrase, we retreated to the car. The road to Mustafakemalpasha was open and we hit it at seventy miles an hour.

Twelve miles from Bursa, where the highway begins to twist through foothills, the western shore of Lake Apolyont sprang into sight at the top of a rise. On Monday, 1 August, its waters were a creamy blue under a hazy sky. Beyond the lake, a line of purple mountains humped into the air and somewhere buried in them was the village of Dorak. It was here, according to Anna Papastrati's notes, that the tombs had been discovered, and among the objects Mellaart had said he had seen in the house in Izmir was a silver-bladed sword on which was etched a line of nine sea-going ships. They were small with high-prancing sterns through which a single large oar protruded to act as a rudder. One of the boats carried a rectangular sail; all of them were being driven forward with banks of oars. Their need in this part of the world was obvious. From the north-west corner of Lake Apolyont, a river ran eleven miles down to the Sea of Marmara. From there access to the Mediterranean lay to the west through the Dardanelles, and to the north-east through the Bosphorus to the Black Sea. Beyond was everywhere. It is possible that the foreign artifacts in the tombs, like the gold fragments which once covered an Egyptian wooden throne and dated the burial in the third millennium, came this way from overseas. At any rate, the people of the Yortan culture were established around this lake; and Troy lay only one hundred miles away.

Thirty-five miles from Bursa, the road swung to the left and skirted the western edge of the lake heading towards Mustafakemalpasha. The sun burned with a rasping heat and the town moved at a casual pace. At the pavement café the black seeds of the water melon covered plate after plate like scattered ink blots, and the tea-seller sat on the kerb. The main street was lined with timber houses and their inhabitants hugged the shadows of the balconies. A donkey flicked flies off its hind legs with a swinging tail and the woman standing by it tugged a veil more securely across her nose. The local prosecutor's office occupied one sector of the police headquarters which lay at the end of a garden cut off from the road by a wall and an iron gate. The officer we were looking for was still at lunch we were told, and so we waited in the car squeezed up against a tree on the edge of a dusty square. The minutes ticked by. Each man who rounded the corner across the street caused a stir, but inevitably he strolled on towards the centre of the town. A stork sailed across the roofs in a never-ending glide as if it were too hot to engage in any muscular effort more than was necessary to clear the gables. At ten-past two, a tall thin figure crossed the square and entered the police station. We gave him three minutes and then followed. An armed policeman stopped us in the main hall and we asked for the public prosecutor. He disappeared into an office on the left and returned to wave us in. The room was quite small with a desk extending from the windows overlooking the garden. Behind it sat our man. In the opposite corner, slumped in an armchair was someone whose whole attitude spoke of an easy acquaintance with the official we had come to see. He was very slim with light-coloured hair. A thin grey bush-shirt covered his shoulders, and his face wore an expression of faint amusement, as though the tail-end of a joke was still lingering in his mind. But the two men really did not matter. On the desk was a large buff envelope, about eight inches wide and eighteen inches long, of great age and torn at the edges. Out of it stuck a pile of documents about three inches thick. It was hard to look elsewhere. We were offered seats, and rude enough not to wait for tea.

'Did Memduh Oktav telephone you . . . ? '

'Yes,' said the prosecutor. 'I had his call just before lunch.'

'I expect he mentioned to you that we were wanting to look at the Dorak dossier.'

'Yes, he did. That's it on the desk.' The stranger in the corner was now smiling broadly. We asked Ayhan Utul to ask as tactfully as he could who this man was.

'I am an advocate in the town,' said the stranger sitting up in his chair. 'But that is not important. I also own the local paper and I heard you were coming here and I thought I might be of some help.'

'That's very kind of you,' we said, lobbing words gently around like partners warming up in a tennis match, 'but how. . . .'

As if on cue, the office door opened and a second stranger stood there hesitantly. He was a plump man in a grey suit and he was sweating.

'This,' said the first man, 'is Ibrahim Erbek. He used to edit a small newspaper in Mustafakemalpasha, but now he works for me.'

'Does he fit into the story in any way?' we asked.

'Oh yes. Do you remember that on the third day of the *Milliyet* stories there was a picture of a man who said he recognised Mellaart?'

We did.

'That's him.'

Ibrahim Erbek nodded eagerly. 'I came along because I thought you might want to see me.'

This rush of volunteers was a bit embarrassing. Something we were not exactly equipped for, conditioned as we were by this time by all the prising open we had had to do. And it was fairly clear, anyway, that Erbek was not exactly comfortable in his new-found role of witness. His editor had obviously ordered him to attend the meeting.

The public prosecutor made the next move. He pushed the

dossier towards the edge of his desk. 'Why don't you take these and look at them. There's an empty room across the corridor. You can take your time in there.'

We picked up the package and followed the policeman down the passage. The room we were to use contained only a long table down the middle and six chairs. Shutters across the open window were pulled tight and through the slats slices of another garden were just visible in a washed-out glare. We sat together on one side of the table. Ayhan Utul, Ibrahim Erbeck and a police officer took seats on the other. The dossier might be ours for the afternoon, but the prosecutor's office was not letting it out of its sight. It lay between us like the ball at a soccer kick-off. It was a moment to take one's time. Like a lover with a girl in his arms and the night before him, it would have been indecent to rush. We took Erbeck first. Sticking out of the dossier anyway, yellow by now, were the familiar newspaper clippings. They pointed the way to the questioning.

'Tell us, Ibrahim Bey, how you got mixed up with this?'

Erbeck launched into an explanation as if heaving himself into a sky-jump.

'I used to edit a newspaper in town. *Ataeli*. It's dead now. One day a jeep drove into town. There were six people in it. It was some kind of official transport. It had a red number plate, that's how you can tell.'

'Who were the people in it?'

'There was a man next to the driver.'

'Describe him.'

'He was medium height, with glasses, and he had light-coloured hair. And there was a woman in front too. She was Turkish. And there were three men in the back, labourers, they were dressed in blue overalls.'

'How did you get to meet them?'

'Well, it was a market day, that would make it a Thursday. And they'd driven in late in the morning and they were asking people in the town if there was coal in the area. They said they were looking for mines. Now, there was a bit of unemployment at the time, and naturally the men were interested in what they were saying. If there was any chance of work, they wanted to know about it. So they brought these people to my office.'

'What year would you say that was?'

'1955 or 1956. I can't remember exactly.' The dates accorded with those *Milliyet* published, if not with its reporter's notes which had stated '1953'.

'What happened when you met them?'

Erbek wiped the sweat off his face with the back of his hand.

'I asked them if they would like lunch. I told them we could have it in my office. I thought they would make a good story. The woman said she thought that was a good idea, and she said she'd like some tomatoes. There was a greengrocer's outside my office and she went out and did some shopping. We sat round my desk and ate tomatoes, grapes and cheese and drank beer.'

'And how did they behave while you had lunch. Were they uneasy or anything?'

'No,' said Erbek. 'The man didn't say much. The woman did all the talking. She spoke to the man in French and, I think, English. I had the impression that the man didn't speak Turkish.'

'But Mellaart does. Say it *was* him. Do you think that he wouldn't have spoken to you in your own language?'

Erbek thought it unlikely.

'What was the woman's French like?'

'Oh, she had a Parisian accent.'

'Then you know what a Parisian accent sounds like?' That would have been a sophisticated item of knowledge for a Turkish journalist in a small town to possess.

Erbek screwed up his eyes, 'Well, she didn't sound like a

Turk speaking French. You know what I mean?' It was clear that to someone like Erbek, anyone speaking another language would be identified with the capital of the country concerned.

Nevertheless, Erbek's observations were interesting. Arlette Mellaart, as a highly educated Turk, speaks fluent French. On the other hand, Mellaart himself is fairly fluent in Turkish and has little need to have things translated for him, not with his facility for foreign languages. And when the two of them are together, they converse in English. We had never heard them speak French to each other.

'Now tell us. How long were they in your office?'

'About two and a half hours.'

'What did you talk about?'

'I asked them what they were. They said they were geologists looking for coal, lignite.'

'Did you believe them?'

'Well, yes,' said Erbek. 'It seemed a reasonable question to ask. There is coal in the area. There used to be some mines in the hills.'

'You haven't told us what the woman looked like. Can you remember?'

Erbek thought for a moment. 'She was wearing a blue linen suit, no sleeves. She was tanned, a Turkish type. She had light brown eyes and fair hair. Well, it might have been chestnut. She was shorter than the man. She came up to my shoulder. And she had white sports shoes, with bandages round them.'

'Any distinguishing marks?'

'Yes. She had a small scar under one eye and a gold tooth.'

'You remember things like that after all these years? It's a long time.'

'When you're a Turk and live in a small town,' said Erbek, 'you remember strangers well.'

'Did you happen to ask them their names?'

'No.'

'You mean there were seven of you sitting in your office for two and a half hours and you didn't ask them their names?'

'It is not a Turkish habit to ask people what they are called,' said Erbek.

'And they left you after lunch?'

'Yes, that's right. They asked for a guide to take them to the coal district, but I couldn't get them one. The man I wanted was busy. You remember, it was market day. I told them the best place to go was to Söğütalan, that's rich in coalmining. But I know they didn't go there. That's the funny thing. As they left I heard them mention Dorak. They found a villager in Mustafakemalpasha and they took him with them.'

The *Milliyet* cuttings came out of the packet. They were, of course, clippings of the anti-Mellaart campaign.

'Now, let's leap on to 1962. You remember you saw this picture of Mellaart in the paper and you came forward to say you had seen him in the town.'

'I didn't,' said Erbek most emphatically.

'You *didn't*. But that's what the paper said, or seemed to say at any rate.'

'No.' Erbek grew excited. 'The reporter came here. You know Turhan Aytul? He came here with the picture and asked me if I knew the man.'

'The caption to the picture says you were "a youth of Mustafakemalpasha".'

'Maybe I was,' said Erbek. 'but I was also the editor of the local newspaper.'

'Did you identify the man in the photograph as Mellaart then?'

'I told him "I'm not dead sure it's Mellaart, it was a long time ago."'

128   THE DORAK AFFAIR

'But you've just described to us in detail how the woman looked and that was even longer ago.'

'I know. I know. But I said to Turhan Aytul, "I'm not sure. I don't know exactly." But when I saw the picture . . .'

'But you're not sure now?'

'I wasn't sure then,' exclaimed Erbek. 'I *told* him I wasn't sure. Anyway, *Milliyet* was wrong. There were many, many mistakes because he changed what was told to him.'

'You're a journalist. Didn't you complain?'

'I did, but it didn't do any good. I even went to Istanbul. You know *Akşam*, the other paper. I had a friend on it who was a columnist. But he couldn't help me.'

There was a long silence. A car roared by in the distance. Everybody by now was sweating, with dark patches oozing across shirt-fronts. The door opened. The public prosecutor was looking in to see how things were going and to ask if we needed drinks. Bottles of lemonade and small glasses of tea were spread over the table, and we drank as though to put out a fire. There remained two final questions.

'Ibrahim Bey, you work on a newspaper and you must have a better knowledge than most how people behave. If you were an archaeologist looking for an illegal dig, something you would have to keep secret, would you drive into a strange town and let yourself wind up in the offices of a local paper? Just the very spot where a man like you looking for news would leap on the story. Would you?'

Erbek shook his head. 'Of course not.'

'But if you *were* a geologist and you were looking for coal, where would you head for in a strange town? What would be the one place likely to have all the information in the district?'

Aydin Dikmen, the jazz-drummer collector of antiquities, displaying an obsidian mirror from Çatal Hüyük, cult objects and figurines from this and other sites.

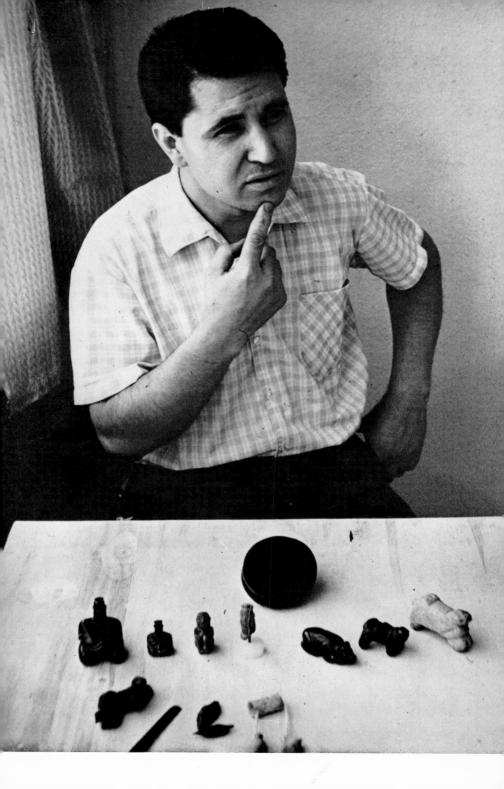

An inhabitant of Hacilar, with gold watch, ring and a camera worn as a status symbol, demonstrates the size of a pot he has hidden away but which will soon be produced for sale

Erbek nodded. 'A newspaper office.'

Despite the closed shutters which kept the room dark, the heat was oppressive. Everyone round the table was sticking to his chair. Erbek wriggled to free himself inside damp clothing, and he wiped his hands together. He had been a good witness. No professional investigator could have asked for better co-operation. The journalist had spoken with a frankness that seemed to suggest the unloading of a burden that he had carried around for years. After all, his appearance at police headquarters was entirely voluntary, unless of course his advocate-editor, for reasons best known to himself, had applied more than a little pressure. All through the interview Erbek spoke with tremendous speed, even at some points anticipating the interpreter to jump in with his answers. Whatever his motives, he gave the impression that an injustice might have been done and this was the one opportunity to put some weight on the other side of the scales. If Erbek was to be believed, his colleague from Istanbul had leapt to conclusions which the evidence did not support. All Erbek's 'ifs' and 'buts' had been abandoned by Turhan Aytul in his *Milliyet* series for the sake of a story unclouded by any shadow of doubt.

Now the time had come to open the Dorak dossier. Perhaps the police had evidence that would confirm or deny Erbek's information. Its papers were fanned across the table. Besides the *Milliyet* cuttings, it contained several sheets that one would expect to find: two copies of Erbek's old newspaper which had picked up the story from Istanbul regardless of the evidence which its own editor had presented to the capital, three photo-copies of the *Illustrated London News*, and a Turkish translation of Mellaart's article in the London publication. There was, however, an additional pile of documents which no-one had seen before. They had been filed in chronological order.

On the top was Mellaart's letter of notification of the Izmir find to the Department of Antiquities. It was dated 3 April, 1959 and did nothing more than say that he had come across two Hacilar pots and 'a rich collection of Yortan metalwork in Izmir'. There followed a letter from the Ministry of Education, the Antiquities department's overlord, dated 14 January, 1960, which, provoked by Mellaart's article in London in the previous November, pointed out to the British Institute of Ankara that Mellaart had given no information of how the Dorak evidence had been obtained and that although the story talked about where the treasure had been found, it said nothing about the people involved.

The Institute had rushed to reply. The very next day it explained its predicament in coming up with a satisfactory answer. Both the head of the Institute and his assistant (Mellaart) were on leave in Britain, said the letter, but they would be back in Ankara after 15 March. In the meantime, it went on, a copy of the Ministry's questions would be sent on to them. It did, however, give the Ministry one clue: it passed on an address, '217 Kazim Dirik street, Izmir'. The fact that the street was to be found in the district of Karşiyaka was, through ignorance, omitted.

Now that its investigations had finally got under way, the Turkish Department of Antiquities was not wasting much time. On 30 January it wrote two letters in connection with the case. The first went to the Governor of Izmir, asking him to check in the city if he could find any evidence of the Dorak treasure's existence. The second was sent to its office in Bursa and wanted to know what it had heard about Dorak.

Both local authority departments were galvanised into action. The Izmir police, in possession by now of the girl's name and her address, reported to the local branch of the Ministry of Education on 10 February. The street, they said, was to be found in a commercial area where there were no private houses. As for the name, a certain Papastrati family dealing in tobacco had lived in Izmir before 1922, but had left for Greece during the War of Independence. The name, they concluded, had been given wrongly in order to 'shield the real purpose of the man'.

By 15 February, Ankara's request for information to Bursa had been passed down the administrative line and the headman of the Dorak district was reporting back to his provincial centre. 'There have been no foreigners in the district,' he wrote, 'perhaps there had been some years ago.' At any rate, there was no sign of recent excavations and no reports of activity in the area. 'There is one ruined area next to Dorak,' he added, 'and during a dig done by the villagers a relief was found and embedded in the wall of a windmill. But notice of this was given to the authorities.' Bursa passed on the news to Ankara.

But there was one item of information produced by a local police chief which had a direct bearing on the case. In his report he explained, '. . . during excavations around Dorak some antiquities were found and these were brought to the Bursa museum.' His next sentence was vital to the Mellaart affair. 'A permit was given one day to a Turkish Member of Parliament *to search for coal*'. If this were correct, and there was no reason to believe otherwise, it would explain the appearance in Mustafakemalpasha of a vehicle with a red number plate, the sign of Turkish officialdom.

The information being fed back to Ankara was certainly not pointing to a snooping Englishman who hung about the Dorak region to pick up a significant and valuable archaeological hoard. On the contrary, it had only conveyed the interest of local villagers in collecting the odd find or two, and confirmed the curiosity of a Turkish politician who was on the prowl for a source of fuel.

As a consequence, by the middle of August, 1960, according to the Dorak dossier, the Director of the Bursa museum was filing a conclusive summary of investigations in which he declared '. . . nobody has come to Dorak to excavate.' And

Turkish security was being even more emphatic. No one, it reported, had been in Mustafakemalpasha on any suspicious errand, and, as far as it could find, there was no evidence that 'any foreigner has come here'. If something like this had happened, it ended, 'they must have come secretly across the lake by boat without being seen.' By 1 September, 1960, it was obvious from the file, Turkish concern about Mellaart's connection with the Dorak discovery had been parked on one side.

The dossier, however, had more information to offer. Its next set of documents had been sparked off by a familiar date —29 May, 1962, the day *Milliyet* launched its campaign against Mellaart, *two and a half years* after the archaeologist's report appeared in London. The appearance of these news- paper articles had sent tremors through the Department of Antiquities in Ankara where its poets, nationalistic execu- tives and pedestrian administrators were hyper-sensitive enough to respond to its implications. The case was reopened even though in the meantime Mellaart had quite happily been allowed to operate in Turkey. Once again, letters from the capital flashed out to the relevant provinces with the inevitable questions. And they provoked the inevitable answers. No-one knew any more than he had already declared. But the Dorak dossier still held one hitherto un- revealed document. This was an affidavit, dated 16 July, 1962, and signed by five Dorak villagers at the Mustafa- kemalpasha police headquarters. Its most important testi- mony read:

'I served as the Mukhtar (headman) of the Dorak village from 1955 to 1958. In 1955 a person named Nadir Mar of Işiklar village came to our village with a foreigner. I was not at the village that day. They claimed they were searching for coal. I heard that they searched for coal between Onaç village and Dorak; in a locality called Kayabaşi fifteen minutes from Dorak; and they went away the same day. I never heard about nor saw any excavations conducted in our village prior to or after the said date. However, in 1962 I read in the newspapers that a treasure had been unearthed at Dorak and smuggled out. I have no information about the incident.'

This statement was signed by the Public Prosecutor, a clerk in his department, and a witness who marked the document with a thumb-print. Four other statements to the police confirmed the headman's report. But as the dossier file thickened, Ankara kept the wheels of its investigation in motion. Even so, nothing more relevant to the case emerged than a letter sent on 6 July, 1963, from Bursa to Izmir. 'Find Anna Papastrati' was the essence of its message; but everyone by now was well aware of the impossibility of that.

The contents of the Mellaart file next made it clear that by 1964 the Turkish enquiries had run out of steam. The police were no longer interested. Mellaart was commuting between London and the house on the Bosphorus quite freely, to be picked up by Turkish Security any time it chose, despite further melodramatic newspaper stories that he had disappeared at crucial moments. If going home to England was 'disappearing', then that is what he had done. The Ministry in Ankara, however, still smarting from the wounds to its prestige, was about to show its dissatisfaction with the results of their own investigations. It was in the spring of 1964 that the Ministry had, for the first time, refused Mellaart permission to dig at Çatal Hüyük, even though the following year it was to retreat from its uncompromising position and agree to open the site for excavation by a team in which Mellaart was only a member, not its leader. It could not give permission, the Ministry had written in 1964, until 'the Dorak affair was cleared up'. The likelihood of that was vanishing fast.

By November, 1965, whatever the Turkish departments concerned might think, the case was closed for good. During that autumn, a new amnesty law had been passed in

Parliament which brought the affair to an irrevocable conclusion. From that moment on, all court cases which involved foreigners in litigation in Turkey were to be dropped. Mellaart's was among them. But it was an act, as it happened, that did the archaeologist little good. If the evidence of the Dorak dossier was to be taken at face value, a court action against Mellaart in which Erbek was called as a witness was unlikely to have proved the Englishman guilty. But now, with the case dropped in fortuitous circumstances, rumour was left to fly around unimpeded. There were, to judge from the file, a few frayed edges to the evidence on record. Who was the 'foreigner' referred to in the Dorak headman's affidavit? Did he mean someone from overseas? Or was it his way of describing a visitor from another region? According to Erbek, a man *and a woman* had appeared in the area on a mysterious mission. On the other hand, the villagers themselves spoke only of *one* stranger. Then again, so the *Milliyet* man had reported, the people of Dorak were quite happy to stand on the very edge of the graves the 'thieves' had excavated; but, so they swore to the police, a single visitor had called there for one day, and he, they added, was looking for something else.

The probabilities, suggested by the dossier, fell into a line that suggested Mellaart's innocence, on this score at least. The questions provoked could only elicit one answer. Would an archaeologist on a rare dig turn up in a strange town with three Turkish labourers in the back seat of a vehicle carrying an official number plate, and not expect to be identified if the need arose? Would such a man sit for two and a half hours in the office of a newspaper editor and expect his real purpose to go unrecognised? Could such a team of six descend on a lonely village and excavate a site without every peasant for a mile around knowing of their presence? The reasonable answer is 'no'. The dig had been scientifically excavated and recorded in meticulous detail in the charred notes that

Mellaart had seen in the Papastrati household. They were not the work of archaeological scavengers. It would have taken days, weeks, to document the riches of the Dorak hoard, and their provenance could be accurately assessed only by carefully relating each artifact to its position in the two tombs. Who was going to do this in a day?

On the other hand, circumstantial evidence pointed to the fact that the strangers in town *were* looking for coal. For a start, they were in the right region of Turkey, where mines had once existed. They had said to various people in Mustafakemalpasha that they were looking for it. Dorak's headman had been told that that was at least one stranger's intention. And the local police chief had recorded that a permit had been given to a Member of Parliament for that very reason. What more could a jury ask?

We were driven back to Bursa that night like a couple of limp sacks. To the right of the road the mountains in which Dorak was hidden were black against a cold moonlit sky. Even Ridvan, our Turkish driver, had somehow caught the mood of exhausted exhilaration which had to attend the examination of the dossier, a file that for so long had hovered on the horizon like some Holy Grail. The feeling of a minor triumph accomplished was an emotion which, we thought, might be indulged. We had set out from London with alternative headlines in mind: Mellaart was a thief or had been victimised. Even now, despite the conclusions to be drawn from the Dorak dossier at Mustafakemalpasha, there were questions remaining to be answered. We talked about them that night over dinner on a terrace overlooking the main street of Bursa. We talked about them too long. Suddenly, it was very late and there was a ferry to be caught at Yalova on the Sea of Marmara, if we were to reach Istanbul that night. Ridvan drove as though Seljuk hordes were on his tail. The headlights of the car picked up one hairpin bend after another as we wove our way on squealing tyres through impassive hills. Just before midnight, the port came into sight. Ridvan screamed through the town, raced down a long pier jutting out into dark waters, and slammed on his brakes on the stern of the ship. And as he did so, a metal bridge arose up behind us and locked us on board. The ferry pulled gently away towards an invisible destination.

'I'm just wondering. I've never really noticed a scar under Arlette's eye. Have you?'

'No. I was just wondering if she's got a gold tooth. Have you spotted it?'

'No, can't say I have.'

'We're going to have to ask her, aren't we?'

'Yes. Toss you for it.'

Chapter 9

A Letter from Anna

The letter had been opened. There was no doubt of it. The top of the airmail envelope had been neatly split along its entire length and then resealed with little attempt to obscure the operation. The letter, from the editor of *The Sunday Times* colour magazine, had arrived from London marked 'To await arrival if necessary', and we picked it up at the reception desk of our hotel. The information it contained was highly confidential. Back in Central Anatolia we had requested London to check on the identity of various international dealers who seemed to be mixed up in smuggling rackets. Our editor, in turn, had cabled four foreign correspondents, and this letter contained entertaining replies from Copenhagen, Rome, Athens and New York. The premature opening could not have been the action of an office secretary. Envelopes are not that scarce, and in any case it is not office practice to send out its correspondence as though it was the work of a blundering five-year-old. Who then had done it? Since the clumsy efforts of the men who were trailing us in Ankara, we had forgotten that we ourselves were the subject of some interest in Turkey. This was a sharp reminder. If Turkish Security had opened the letter, it now possessed a lot of information which we could not publish in view of our own libel laws, but which the Turks would no doubt be happy to have. There could come a day when one of these dealers might present himself at the frontier. It was going to be hard luck on him if he did.

Our reaction was one of amusement more than anything, but there seemed no harm in letting other Turkish government departments know what their colleagues were up to, and we made contact with the friend in the Ministry of Tourism. We told her of our suspicions.

'That's funny,' she said.

'What's funny about it?'

'I had a phone call about you this morning.'

'Who from?'

'Let me tell you what happened. There was a man on the other end of the line. He said you were expected back in Istanbul and did I know where you had been when you went south. I said I didn't. He then went on to ask if I knew what you had been finding out. I told him I didn't know that either ... and then suddenly I realised I didn't know who I was speaking to, so I said "Who's that?" ... and the line went dead.

'Who do you think it was?' we asked.

'I don't know,' our friend replied somewhat tentatively. 'Perhaps it was the same people.'

'Well, unless Turkish Security is like our own Intelligence departments who keep things so secret they have to spy on each other, your agents must know where we've been and what we've been doing.'

'In that case,' she said, 'it might have been another newspaper.'

'Oh God, not *Milliyet* again? Well, they can go and jump in the Bosphorus.'

They didn't, in fact; they turned up at the hotel. Mehmet Ali Birand, *Milliyet's* distinguished diplomatic editor, had brought with him a reporter from the news desk and a young photographer. It was apparent that Mehmet Bey had been left uneasy at the situation which had arisen between his own

paper and Mellaart, and this looked like an attempt to combine news-gathering with a conciliatory gesture. No blame
for what had happened in the past or what might happen in
the future can be attached to Birand. All along, he acted in
good faith. But there is a Turkish proverb which fitted this
occasion admirably. *'Armut piş ağzima düs'* ('When the pear
is cooked it falls into the mouth'). And we had the pear, and
Milliyet was sitting there with its mouth wide open.

Mehmet Ali indicated the journalist on his right. 'My
friend thought perhaps you would like to tell us something
about your travels. You know . . . what you have found.'

'You're not serious?' we asked.

Mehmet Ali laughed self-consciously. 'Well, perhaps a
little something?'

The situation was ludicrous. 'Are you really suggesting
that our paper should spend hundreds of pounds to send us
on a story halfway across the world, and then when we've
dug for the facts, we just hand them all over to you?'

The diplomatic editor translated for his colleagues. They
saw the joke, too, and asked if we would like a drink. We
went on chatting together for about a quarter of an hour,
gently fending off a few probing questions, while the photographer snapped away in the hotel bar to illustrate an article
on us which Mehmet Ali promised would not appear until
we had left Turkey. It was difficult to condition ourselves to
the workings of a young Press which still thought visiting
journalists made news.

But if the *Milliyet* team was a little coy about its first
audacious request, its second left them even more actively
hopping from one foot to the next.

'When are you going to see Mr Mellaart again?' asked the
reporter.

'This afternoon as it happens, why?'

'We are wondering if we can come out with you and
interview him?'

'That seems very unlikely, considering what you people have been writing about him.'

'Perhaps this time it would help him,' explained Mehmet Ali. 'We only want to ask him a question or two and get the facts straight. Do you think he would object to that?'

'Most strongly. You know that facts have a way of not getting published the way they come out. . . . But we mustn't interfere with what you want to do. The least we can do is ask him. Let's telephone and see what happens.'

While Mehmet Ali had been speaking, it had occurred to us that their assignment might do something to feed a little more of the truth to Turkish public opinion coloured for so long by newspaper reports. It seemed unlikely that now *Milliyet* knew we had seen the dossier and they had not, that they would stay out on the limb of suggestive reporting. And an ill-advised thought that turned out to be.

However, we called the house at Kanlica, and Arlette Mellaart answered the phone. We explained the request, and as expected her reaction was one of outright refusal. 'You know what they'll do,' she said.

'But supposing you were to agree, and the interview was held in front of witnesses, don't you think that would do some good?'

Mrs Mellaart could be heard discussing the proposal with her husband.

'When would they come?' she asked.

'This afternoon.'

'Would you come with them?'

'If you wish.'

'You know, the two Frenchmen will be here as well. They are just finishing their film.'

'Good. Ask them to sit in as well. And anyone else you can lay your hands on.'

'All right,' she said, a little reluctantly. 'We shall expect you.'

Back in the bar, we gave the *Milliyet* team the conditions of the interview, and they accepted them. We arranged to leave together for Kanlica after lunch.

The meeting that took place that afternoon was in fact our second encounter with Mellaart since our return to Istanbul. The first had been arranged to re-check his story and to confront the archaeologist with what new details had been discovered on the tour through Anatolia. By now, Mellaart must have been pushed to the limits of his endurance by the persistent interrogations, but he gave little sign of losing his patience. Having committed himself to telling the story in full for the first time, he appeared satisfied to see the job through to the bitter end. And no one, least of all himself, could tell how bitter, if bitter, it would be.

The renewed questioning had not been easy. Most of it involved presenting Mellaart with stories against himself, some of which were built round intensely personal revelations. But if he suspected that we had now come into knowledge which he himself had consciously kept secret, there was no sign of apprehension. On the contrary, the archaeologist was in an affable mood.

'We're getting very popular,' said Arlette, as she greeted us off the boat. 'Jimmie's now got someone coming from America to see him. Have you heard of Joseph Alsop? He's very good, isn't he? Well, he's written to say that he is writing a long article for *The New Yorker* on the Neolithic, and he would like to call here and then go on to Çatal Hüyük with us. He wants us to take him over the site. That's good, isn't it?'

For the Mellaarts, it was indeed. That made the third set of journalists independently to have come across the significance of this particular excavation. Archaeology was not Alsop's main work as a writer, but an interest he indulged at least once a year. His holidays abroad are usually spent in an

area of the world noted for its antiquarian value, and these
trips often result in articles of great length, elegant style and
worthy scholarship.

There was nothing sinister of course in this widespread
concern in the work of Mellaart. When Columbus discovered
America, it is a safe guess that the news travelled beyond the
court of Spain. But the world's interest in Mellaart has
always been taken by the Turkish Press as a sign that there is
an evil conspiracy afoot. Its paranoic reaction has led it into
wild accusations unsupported by the smallest shred of evidence. There was, for instance, an extraordinary outburst in
May, 1965, from *Yeni Tanin*, a popular daily published in
Ankara. After the usual opening machine-gun burst aimed
straight at Mellaart, the article launched into a series of
loaded questions unparalleled in their implications. A few of
them are worth looking at.

'Why was Mellaart thrown out of the Institute in Ankara,
and then protected by being given a job in the University of
Istanbul?' demanded the newspaper.

(Mellaart's term of office had come to an end in Ankara,
and he was given a temporary post at the university when a
change of government and a purge removed several of the
academy's professors.)

'Why do journalists abroad always write about Hacilar
and Çatal Hüyük *repeatedly*. Is this not a sort of pressure to
help Mellaart in Turkey?'

(At that date, no journalists anywhere had written at
length about those two places. And even if they had, it is
unlikely that it was done to influence the Turkish government; always assuming that by this means it *is* possible to
exert this kind of influence.)

'Why does the *Illustrated London News* always come back
to the same thing?'

(Poor old *I.L.N.* But then on countless occasions in its
traditional coverage of the world's archaeology, it is often to

be found returning to a site at the end of another season's dig. That's just good journalism.)

But the plot, according to *Yeni Tanin*, was thickening. 'What is the relationship that British Petroleum has with the British archaeologist?' cried the author.

('One year at a dig,' says Mellaart, 'they lent us an old Daimler for transport. It used to do about fifteen miles an hour and was often passed by donkeys.')

The writer was warming to his task. In the distance, you can almost hear the shout, 'And furthermore...' What, he asked, 'is the connection between Unilever and Mellaart?'

(A representative of the giant corporation once contributed to a season's excavation costs the sum of 200 Turkish lire—£8.)

The reporter wound himself for his final fling. 'Who,' he thundered, 'are those people who give financial help to Mellaart and do not give their names?'

(And one thinks of all those gentle old ladies of Cheltenham or Hackensack who might unwittingly fall under this heading by anonymously donating a small contribution to an excavation fund.)

Yeni Tanin's performance was more impressive for its tone of implied invective than for the depth of its research. What the Turkish Press would make of Joseph Alsop's visit, one shuddered to think. What it did do in fact, as its actions later revealed, was characteristic. But for the moment Mr Alsop could take care of his own story: ours required immediate agreement or denial.

Once again, we were sitting on the quayside watching flocks of sheerwaters skimming the surface of the Bosphorus as they flew north-east towards the Black Sea. The questioning was spasmodic, a timing dictated by the heat of the sun, or perhaps by the desire to catch a man off his guard.

'Jimmie, when we were in Ankara, we had a long chat with Seton Lloyd and among the many things he told us, he said that when the balloon went up he told you and Arlette to take the Institute Land Rover and go and look at Dorak. He said that as you'd seen the treasure, you might as well find the place it came from.'

'That's right,' said Mellaart.

'That would be in 1960 . . . 1960 . . . the date's important.'

'That would be about it.'

'What happened?'

'Well, we drove there from Ankara, through Mustafa-kemalpasha, and up into the hills. The going was rough and it was getting dark when we got near the place. And we decided we couldn't get any closer with the vehicle, so we got out and looked down towards the lake. We couldn't see any sign of the excavations from where we were, but we could see where they might be.'

'You weren't any more certain than that?'

'No.'

'Did you see or speak to anyone while you were up there?'

'Yes . . . there was an old man with a donkey who came by. We talked to him for a bit. We came back after that and told Seton Lloyd what had happened.'

'You'd swear that you never went into the village?'

'Yes,' said Arlette.

'Can you be sure about the date though?'

Mrs Mellaart disappeared into the house for a few minutes and then came out with a batch of small diaries. 'Yes,' she said, turning the pages over,' that would be the year. We were away from 25 June to 27 June.'

'While we were at the Institute,' we went on, 'Seton Lloyd made one very peculiar remark. He said that some time after your recreations of the Dorak artifacts had been published, his wife asked you if she could have another look at your original sketches. She wanted to check on something she was not too happy about, and you told her that you had destroyed them, thrown them away. I must say at the time we all thought that was a very odd thing to do. Did you in fact?'

Mellaart looked incredulous.

'Then you've still got them?'

'Yes. Yes. They're in my office in the Institute of Archaeology in London.'

'Do ... do you think we could see them when we get back?'

'Of course you can. The office will probably be locked, but I'll give you a letter of introduction to the porter at the front door, and he'll let you in.' As good as his word, the archaeologist went into his study and typed the necessary permission at once, as though by this immediate act to affirm the existence of the drawings. We tucked the letter safely away for use as soon as we got to London.

'You know, before we left here for Ankara, you said something about writing to Anna Papastrati to get hold of the photographs she'd promised you. How many times did you write to her?'

'About two.'

'And got no reply?'

'No,' said Mellaart, puffing fiercely on his cigarette. 'Not to those requests, anyway. But you know I told you that she had written to me at the Institute, giving me permission to go ahead and publish my account of the treasure. I remember I told you that I thought at first it was in answer to my letters. But then I thought later that she could have just written it out of the blue without ever getting my letters to her. I told you that.'

'Yes, that's quite right ... er ... did you keep the letter?'

Mellaart looked at us for some time. '... Yes.'

'Could we see it, do you think?'

Again Mellaart sat staring, slumped in his chair. He remained motionless with a blue haze of tobacco smoke drifting around his ears. Then, suddenly, he leapt to his feet and marched into the house. His wife followed him. The air was quite still. Three minutes later, the archaeologist reappeared in the garden doorway, paused for a moment, and then, walking a few paces forward, threw a piece of paper onto a table.

'There,' he said, with the faintest tremor in his voice, 'Now you know everything.'

In front of us, if the document was genuine, was one more clue to the girl's existence. The name 'Anna Papastrati', in a distinctively flamboyant handwriting, rounded off the end of a short typed letter. Her permission had been composed on a plain sheet of paper on the left side of which two holes had been punched for filing. And it read:

> Miss Anna Papastrati
> Kazim Direk Caddesi no.
> 217
> Karsiyaka—Izmir.

> 18/10/1958

Dear James,
Here is the letter you want so much.
As the owner, I authorise you to publish your drawings of the Dorak objects, which you drew in our house. You always were more interested in these old things than in me!
Well, there it is. Good luck and goodbye.
Love,
Anna Papastrati

James Mellaart Esq.
Ingiliz Arkeolöji Enstitüsü
Ankara.

From what seemed years back, one recalled Seton Lloyd's first mention of Dorak and the girl . . . 'he was having a ding-dong. . . .' Plainly, if with more delicacy, this was to be read into those lines. But the letter from first glance could be construed in two ways. If it was the real thing, Mellaart and Anna Papastrati had shared a relationship which was something more than a passing acquaintance. The 'goodbye' had such a final ring. And if all this was true, it went a long way to explaining the archaeologist's embarrassment at producing the evidence and his reluctance to go too deeply into the story whenever he repeated it to others. On the other hand, if it were a forgery to cover the real circumstances in which the hoard had been found or even somehow to substantiate the treasure's existence, it raised a good many questions of a peculiar nature. If a man had need to fake the letter, to explain the otherwise inexplicable, why should he compose one which would set in train a series of prognostications which in themselves might prove even more embarrassing? Would a man, to reinforce his reputation, invent an affair that never took place? Stranger things have been done; but in these circumstances, one wonders.

By the time Mellaart alleges he met the girl in Izmir, he had been married just four years. It is not unlikely then that, when he received permission to publish in Ankara, he would tell his chief a story to disguise the fact that he had met the girl so recently. It was only after he had discussed with his wife how he had come across the Dorak finds that he changed his account to Seton Lloyd. He had no need to go back on his first story unless his conscience was troubling him. It seemed it did.

It had cost Mellaart a great deal to show that letter to strangers for the first time. He had uncovered an intimate detail of his private life and the experience was patently disturbing. A smart change of subject that would put him on surer ground was called for.

'Jimmie. One thing we must confirm with you. According to *Milliyet* the crooks were in the Dorak area in 1955 or 1956.

Now they identified you with them, but did they ever ask you where you were in those years?'

'No. They never asked me, so I never thought to tell them.'

'So let's go through your alibi again?' we said.

It was a conveniently timed request. The archaeologist's wife consulted her diaries.

'Yes, here it is,' she said. 'That was the year you were digging at Beycesultan.'

'Of course,' chipped in Mellaart. 'I remember. Seton Lloyd was in charge of the dig and we left Ankara by car at the end of April. As a matter of fact, we had an accident just outside the city and Seton Lloyd was nearly killed. I took over the site for the season.'

'That's right,' confirmed Arlette, 'and you finished work there on 6 July and came straight back to Ankara. I was expecting a baby. Alan was born the next day.'

'And did you leave the site while you were there?' we asked.

'No.'

'Would you have any witnesses to check that you were there all the time?'

Mellaart reeled off a string of names. 'What does that make? Seven English archaeologists and a Turkish government representative.'

'Did you leave the house in Ankara after that?'

'No,' said Mellaart, I'd hardly be likely to do that and leave Arlette with a tiny baby.'

'Right. That takes care of 1955. What about 1956?'

Arlette turned the pages of her diary. 'That was your second year at Beycesultan. You were there till the end of July again. . . .'

'. . . and then we had to move to Istanbul,' interrupted Mellaart. 'I had three thousand books to shift and that took a bit of doing. I haven't finished sorting them out yet. I've still got some rubbish here. Anyway, that took up the rest of the summer.'

Ankara is two hundred and seventy-five miles from Dorak; not, one would think, a distance to be lightly travelled twice in three days, especially if an archaeological site had to be excavated in the middle of it with any scientific care. Only dynamite would have done the job in the time; and that has yet to be recommended as an archaeological technique. This hypothetical period, we reasoned, was the time during which the Mellaarts had been known to visit Dorak—between 25 June and 27 June, 1960. As for Beycesultan, that was an Early Bronze Age site near the town of Uşak, two hundred miles by the best road south of Lake Apolyont. Mellaart's alibis, taken at face value, were reasonably tight.

That night at Kanlica the party was joined by the French team of journalists for dinner. Their work was almost over and they were beginning to unwind. The wine and the raki and the archaeologist's release of tension, now that the worst of the questioning seemed to be over, put hosts and guests in a high-spirited frame of mind. Once again, the sounds of jazz floated across the water. The night appeared to be centrally heated, as the meal was served by servants on the private quayside. Kadri Cenani, Mellaart's father-in-law, was reminiscing about his ancestors and their service at the court of the Sultan in Istanbul.

'It is such a coincidence,' he laughed, 'but do you know that it was one of my relations who signed the permit for Schliemann to dig at Troy, and he walked off with all the gold. Now, Jimmie is accused of doing something similar. Of course, it's preposterous.'

Gold? We looked at each other and remembered Erbek's description of the woman he had entertained in his office in Mustafakemalpasha. The mood was right for the question.

'Arlette.'

'Yes.'

'Look straight at me.'

She giggled. 'What on earth for?'

'Never mind that for the moment. Just look straight at me.'

She leaned across the table, her face frowning with curiosity.

'There. How's that?'

There were no scars to be seen anywhere below her eyes. 'Now open your mouth wide.'

'What for?' She tried, but it was difficult to do that and laugh at the same time. Eventually, she succeeded.

'I can't quite see round at the back. Have you got any gold teeth?'

'Good Lord no. What a funny question to ask.'

We explained what Erbeck had said. She opened her mouth even wider. 'Have a good look,' she managed to gasp. 'There's not a gold tooth in my head.'

'Then it was not likely to have been you in Erbek's office.'

'Perhaps it was the famous Anna?'

'Hardly,' we said. 'According to the "youth" she was a mature woman, somewhere in her thirties we gathered. And by our reckoning and Jimmie's description of her when they met, she would have been about eighteen in 1955. So it wasn't her either.'

'Then who the hell was it?' Kadri Cenani asked. But no-one seemed to care.

Later that night, when the Frenchmen had left and the air had cooled a little, the Mellaarts and ourselves were drinking in the study, and *still* the story the archaeologist had told to Seton Lloyd in Ankara was at the back of our minds.

'You know, that was a heck of a lie you told about finding the Dorak stuff six years before. Why did you feel you had to do it. It wasn't exactly designed to inspire confidence in your second version. If you'd told one, you could easily tell another.'

Mellaart took a quick look at his wife.

'I know how Jimmie felt,' said Arlette.

'You know, I was damned frightened that she might get scared suddenly and whip all the stuff away,' said Mellaart, shifting uneasily in his chair.

'You had to be nice to her, didn't you Jimmie?' explained Arlette.

'Put yourselves in my place. This was a very valuable find. I knew I wasn't going to get all that much time to take a note of it. What could I do? I had to keep her happy. . . .' His voice died slowly.

'Jimmie did the only thing he *could* do.' Arlette was smiling at her husband. 'You had to be nice to her.'

Nine people were sitting round the large table in the shuttered room at Kanlica. The *Milliyet* team had arrived to interview Mellaart in front of witnesses, as we had arranged on the telephone. The company consisted of the archaeologist, his wife, Kadri Cenani, the two Frenchmen—Jean Vidal and René Dazy, Mehmet Ali Birand, the reporter Mektup Yazdim, aud ourselves. Yazdim carried his own camera and took a few pictures of Mellaart on the terrace after his cross-examination in the house. The questioning went over the usual ground, and Mellaart alone answered the queries, with just an aside or two from his wife and father-in-law. The rest sat silent. The atmosphere during the interview was one of rigid politeness, and though old sores were being scraped, Mellaart behaved throughout with absolute correctness. On the basis of one's hindsight, it would be easy to read into the proceedings what was not then readily apparent. One recalls, however, Arlette Mellaart's first reaction. 'You know what they'll do.' The whole area was covered: the girl on the train, the stay in Izmir, the disappearance of both girl and house, and so on. But Yazdim was very particular about one fact: the date when the Mellaarts had driven to the Dorak region.

What, then, was there to feel apprehensive about? It was almost impossible not to become involved in this incident, although we had to accept that other journalists were doing just what we had done. But as much as one fought to stay neutral, the outcome of this interview was enough to provoke the most partisan response. It was as if no witnesses had ever been present.

Although the publication in *Milliyet* of this final confrontation between the pursued and the pursuers was published outside the chronology of this investigation, this is the appropriate point to examine its worst excesses.

In the first place, in an introduction above the headline, the archaeologist is referred to as 'Mellaart the "mysterious" —as in police films'. An equivocal statement perhaps, but not one stepping beyond the bounds of licence. Next, the headline quotes Mellaart himself: 'The £48 million treasure is still in Turkey.' Lesson: never let a good headline out of your sight no matter how demonstrably untrue it is. The subheadline moved on a little: 'The British archaeologist who revealed the existence of the Dorak treasure still excavates in Anatolia.' The implication is obvious, and a short telephone call to Ankara would have put the facts straight. The introduction to the article itself was an astonishing appeal to self-justification. We were flattered. The *Sunday Times* team was mentioned as being present at the interview as if this converted what followed into Holy Writ.

The first point at issue, it is true, arose some way down the text. But its validity is in no doubt. 'Was Anna Papastrati aware of the value of the objects?' asks the reporter. 'Yes,' says Mellaart in the *Milliyet* account. In fact he said 'No' and there are, excluding his wife and father-in-law, four witnesses to say so. 'According to you, had the woman any knowledge of archaeology?' is the next question. Mellaart is made to say 'Possibly, yes'. In fact, again he said 'No'. Somewhat later, the account goes on, 'According to you, has the Dorak treasure been smuggled out of the country?' . . . 'No', Mellaart is supposed to have said, 'it is in Turkey and cannot possibly have been smuggled out as I would have been contacted as the specialist.' What Mellaart did say was that there was no evidence of its having been smuggled out. He also went on to say in the interview proper that if it was discovered elsewhere, it could be reclaimed by Turkey on the authority of his original publication.

But, it must be admitted, the twists that appeared in this published report have been quoted out of order. The last two have been isolated as supreme examples of what suggestive writing can achieve. At one point, as we have said, Mektup Yazdim asked the Mellaarts if they had been to Dorak. Their answer was to agree, *in 1960*. However, the *Milliyet* account reads thus: 'Did you ever go to Dorak?' . . . 'Yes, the Director of the Institute, Lloyd, wanted me to go to Dorak so I went with my wife.' . . . 'In this case,' comments the reporter in *Milliyet*, 'what the headman (he mentions a more recent village leader) says is true.' By this blatant omission of the all-important date, the whole emphasis of the reporter's comment is thrown onto the fact that the Mellaarts might have been there *at any time. Even in 1955 or 1956.*

The article wound up, however, with an innuendo that would not be permitted under any civilised acceptance of what is fair comment. It concludes with a Mellaart statement, 'I would like to see the whole business cleared up and closed.' What followed was Yazdim's very articulate comment: a query sign and an exclamation mark. One felt on reading it that one had been visiting another planet.

There were more things to do, though, in Istanbul than to act as referees in a contest of accusation and counter-accusation. Our own investigations had to lead us to one more witness to events. One of the most distinguished private collectors of antiquities in Turkey is a store-owner who deals in fabrics. His shop on one of the main thoroughfares in the city sells a range of materials that appeals to both the domestic consumer and the tourist. His name is Hüseyin Kocabaş, and he is respected throughout the academic archaeological world as the profoundly knowledgable owner of a priceless collection. And there is no doubt that, according to Turkish law, his artifacts have been acquired in a most honourable fashion. But by the mere fact that he is registered as a private collector, he must, by his own nation's legislation, open his museum to public inspection for a certain time each week. It was thus, and because of rumours we had heard, that we presented ourselves at the shop to meet him. A great deal of negotiation ensued, but in the end a date to rendezvous at his home was arranged.

On the day of the interview, we were driven across Istanbul through one of its more prosperous districts to the apartment of the textile merchant. The blocks of flats, for all their Mediterranean ambiance, might well have existed in Mayfair or the better parts of Manhattan. Hüseyin Bey welcomed us at the door of a very well shaded flat. He was wearing a baggy pair of trousers and a white shirt whose neck had been tucked in to reveal a vest. A few strands of hair were brushed across the top of his head and his chin was roughly shaven. From the evidence on his desk, we had interrupted him in the middle of some work of restoration. Under the window at the back of the apartment lay a white wooden frame which contained part of a heavily decorated Ottoman tile. Kocabaş had been painting the continuation of its Turkish design on to the plaster cast which filled up the rest of the square. He was a proud man. With great courtesy, he explained the contents of the various show-cases which lined every wall in the flat. His collection was as comprehensive as any amateur curator could have wished. Room by room he showed us over the antiquities he had bought: there they were: Greek, Roman, Assyrian, Lydian, Hittite, Byzantine; objects, almost without exception, of incredible beauty. And as if to verify in our eyes his reputation in the world outside Turkey, he opened books and catalogues by foreign writers who had published photographs of key works in his collection. There was, however, one display case that he was reluctant to discuss in any great detail, and this contained an exhibition of Neolithic objects. It was, however, of some importance to our story. Mellaart had visited this flat some years before, and recollected that on that occasion he had counted Kocabaş to be in possession of just two pots and one goddess from Hacilar. This was why Mellaart had called at the apartment: to examine objects from his own excavations that he had never seen. But now that we were in the flat, it seemed the time for a recount to judge by the packed disposition of the artifacts in that particular case. And so one of us kept the collector in conversation, while the other did his arithmetic. There had obviously been a bull market in the Neolithic field: the case now contained *fifty-eight Hacilar pots and six goddesses*.

'Hüseyin Bey, you've got a fine collection of stuff over here. Is it easy to come by?' we asked.

'No,' said the textile merchant, 'it is very difficult.'

'But you obviously have a good source of supply.'

'Well, it turns up every now and then.'

'Where did you get most of this then?'

'I deal with a man called Çetinkaya.'

'Şevket Çetinkaya?'

'Yes, that's right. You know him?'

'Sort of.'

Most private collectors in Turkey have a comfortable excuse to account for the extent of their acquisitions. 'If we don't buy what is dug up,' they say, 'then it will only go abroad through international dealers and finally appear in foreign museums.' And they are right. In this wide open market in a world with an insatiable appetite for the rare and the beautiful, the goods will go to the highest bidder. It is an inevitable consequence of the irregular disposition of wealth. In the West, museums may complain of their lack of purchasing funds, but the tears they shed are nothing compared with the weeping east of Istanbul, where government officials can only offer the price of a lollipop for a jumbo-sized, gilt-edged, multi-centred box of chocolates; and the situation can never be corrected while the penalties imposed by Turkish laws for stealing antiquarian objects of great value remain ludicrously small. What can a day or two in prison or a fine of a few pounds mean in terms of the worth of a goddess who was moulded seven thousand years ago? Its effect has been to depress most of the country's museum officers as each year brings news from abroad of the appearance on the scene of even more Turkish treasures. If many of these men are embittered, it is understandable.

There is in Istanbul, however, a conservationist in the city's archaeological museum who bears the pain with patient resignation. Nezih Firatli is a gentle, quiet-voiced curator who works to restore in jig-saw fashion the shattered artifacts that do stay in the country. But even he, despite his mellow temperament, pleads with passion for some sort of action.

'I have given up hope for Turkey,' he said one day as we drank tea in his office. 'You *must* write your story. Perhaps UNESCO will see it and arrange some kind of international agreement. If not, everything will be gone. In ten years' time in Turkey there will be nothing.'

And he further illustrated the depths of his emotions by relating a true anecdote which he clearly looked on as a kind of blazing symbol for all who combined patriotism and pride in safeguarding the nation's inheritance.

He told the story of Osman Hamdi Bey, the founder of Firatli's own museum. Just before the first world war, the Kaiser, on a visit to what was then the Turkish capital, admired in Osman's museum the Alexander sarcophagus, a magnificent tomb, exquisitely carved, which probably had nothing to do with the Greek emperor who died in Babylon. 'It is beautiful,' said the Kaiser, and promptly hinted that it would probably look even better in Berlin. Covetousness such as this was no new phenomenon in the world of archaeology. Professor Machteld Mellinck of Bryn Mawr, discussing once the wholesale seizure of Mediterranean antiquities in the nineteenth century, spoke of 'Western museums (which) . . . rivalled each other in offering them protective custody.' The Kaiser had no wish to change the image. And so it was that one day Osman Hamdi Bey heard that his Sultan was intending to give away his prize exhibit to cement international relations. The founder of the museum went at once to the royal palace. 'Kill me,' he said very bravely to the Sultan. 'If you are going to send my sarcophagus to Berlin, kill me and send my body in it.' The tomb was never moved.

The Turkish end of the Mellaart investigation had been reached. Nothing remained now but to fly back to London and, removed from the feverish atmosphere which surrounded the research, to transform a brief-case of notes into a coherent document in which the evidence would be displayed in as unbiased a form as it was possible to achieve. But it wasn't the end of the story. Neither of us then had any idea how two meetings in England were to offer hints of a solution to the Dorak mystery and throw light on yet another smugglers' route that passed through Istanbul. There were no thoughts of the possibility of widening our area of knowledge as we stood in the dimmed foyer of Yeşilköy airport at four o'clock in the morning, embracing Turkish friends in a clumsy attempt to thank them for all their help. There was, however, just one final wry note which hinted at those other Turks who had seemed to hover in the shadows checking our movements through two thousand miles of Anatolia. It fell neatly into the pattern of those moments when one knew one was not unobserved: the heads poised to overhear in the

Ankara hotel, the protocol official who so inelegantly trailed us, the opened letter in Istanbul.

'Your passports, please,' said the officer behind the counter. A formality; a gesture we had performed many times before.

But now he said, 'Excuse me'. And he walked off with the documents across the deserted stone floors of the terminal building. We waited on a bench for fifteen minutes before he returned and handed back our passports duly stamped. 'Thank you,' he said.

Twenty minutes later, the plane roared up into the night away from the dawn to cross the Sea of Marmara and head towards Athens.

'What do you think went on down there then?'

'He was a long time.'

'I bet they were doing all kinds of checking.'

'Can you see a little man on the phone right now talking to his superior in the city?'

'I wonder what's the Turkish for "Thank Allah, that lot's gone".'

Chapter 10

The Transporter

The porter at the Institute of Archaeology in London, where Mellaart teaches during winter and spring and where we had heard him lecture, stood behind his desk in the foyer and read the letter of introduction the archaeologist had given us. He folded it up and returned it to the envelope.

'Would you like to come with me. I'll open his office for you.'

The room, overlooking the gardens of the square, appeared to have been abandoned in great haste. All its furniture had been pushed into one corner and the floor was littered with cardboard boxes every one of which contained broken pottery. None of it had come from Mellaart's Anatolian sites. The sherds fell into another field of his studies. Under the windows, a working desk extended from wall to wall and this was covered with numerous files. On the left of the door, shelves reaching to the ceiling were packed with books on a score or more aspects of Mellaart's work.

A quick glance round the office showed that what we were searching for was not in sight, and we began a systematic exploration of all cupboards and drawers. Mostly, these contained box after box of colour transparencies which the archaeologist had taken to record his excavations. Otherwise, they housed more books and files. But suddenly, Mellaart's vehement denial in Istanbul that he had destroyed his original evidence began to mean something. There, in a cupboard under the windows, was a shallow cardboard box which held a thick typescript and sheet upon sheet of sketchy drawings. We knew the images by heart. It was the Dorak material.

First of all we examined the typescript. At a rough glance it was about 60,000 words long and recorded in a series of chapters the physical description and provenance of all the objects that were said to have come out of the two tombs. If this were a genuine document, the scholarship was impressive. For page after page, it analysed and synthesised every aspect of the excavation. There was not a detail that did not appear to make sense in the context of the book's thesis. It contained, moreover, one chapter that had been written by another hand. This had been compiled by the colleague of Mellaart who, that winter of 1958 in Ankara, had helped the archaeologist to sort the material into some sort of order before it was presented to Seton Lloyd for the first time. This chapter, too, fitted neatly into the story Mellaart was trying to tell and in every way was consistent with the narrative. The typescript had remained in that box ever since its completion, when Mellaart's superiors had declined to assist its publication until its author could produce *photographic* evidence to substantiate his claims. And this, as everyone well knew, had never been forthcoming.

But if there were no photographs to back the discovery, the sketches in that box seemed to suggest contact with a unique find. The care with which they were drawn was astonishing. On sheets of thin paper, some of it cut from the Ankara Institute's notepaper, Mellaart had pencilled jewelled dagger handles, every gem of which appeared to be exactly in place. There were drawings of an ancient comb with a dolphin motif, of jewel boxes again decorated with dolphins, of a vase in the shape of a bird of gold and silver; there were sketches of the gold leaf covering which was said to have extended over the surface of the wooden throne which could have been a present from Egypt, details of the rug which had

Kazim Direk Street, Izmir. Now called 1777 and 1775 Street

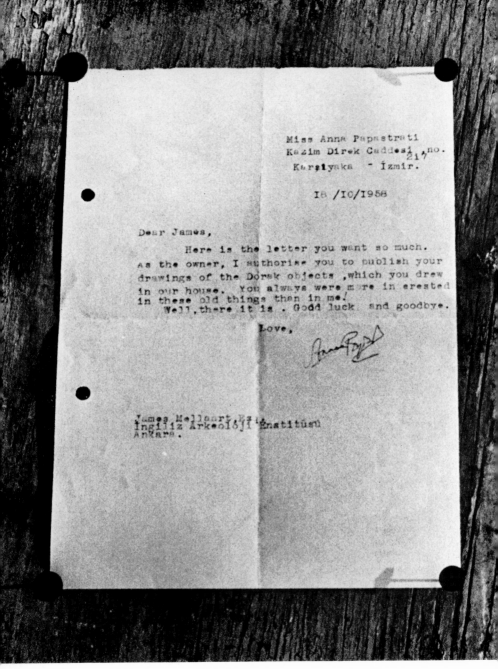

Miss Anna Papastrati
Kazim Direk Caddesi, no. 217
Karşıyaka - İzmir.

18 /10/1958

Dear James,

Here is the letter you want so much.
As the owner, I authorise you to publish your
drawings of the Dorak objects ,which you drew
in our house. You always were more interested
in these old things than in me!
Well,there it is . Good luck and goodbye.

Love,

James Mellaart, Esq.
İngiliz Arkeoloji Enstitüsü
Ankara.

The letter with permission to publish news of the Dorak
treasure, which is said to have been sent by Anna Papastrati

disintegrated when the tombs had been opened, and even *rubbings* of the sword blade etched with ships and of a sherd of alabaster which had been marked with hieroglyphics. And every one of these drawings had been annotated in Mellaart's hand. Written on these sheets and arrowed to the appropriate spots were words and phrases like 'hilt of iron sword', 'crystal', 'extremely like other head', 'length 76 cm', and 'edge of scratch break here'. If Mellaart had done this work at the house in Izmir in the time he claimed, there is every chance that he could not have left the premises if he hoped to complete his task under the continual threat that the girl might suddenly get cold feet. What part all this evidence could play in unravelling the mystery, we shall examine presently. In the meantime, there were other men to talk to.

Museum acquisition is a subject veiled in secrecy. All round the world there is a gentleman's agreement not to discuss in public the means by which new archaeological artifacts are obtained, and this curious code of honour obscures many a route from the sites themselves to the corner of a museum shelf. The reason for this is obvious. While many genuine and nationally controlled excavations are all the time bringing to the surface pots, inscriptions, jewellery and grave goods which add one more item of knowledge to our understanding of cultural growth, the clandestine market in a good many more is a second best method, sometimes the best, of adding to a museum's trophies. All museums trade regularly with the top international dealers whose eyes are skinned for a bargain, but very few museum officials will question the recognised dealer who brings to them a particularly valuable item. The trader's honesty is accepted in good faith, but there seems no reason why it should be. If there appears on the market a significant piece of pottery from, say, Greece, Egypt or Turkey, and the artifact has the value of being unique or extremely rare, it can have appeared only by being taken across its 'home' frontier illegally. National antiquity laws ensure that. Of course, the dealers have their excuses. Most of them will tell you, if pressed sufficiently, that the object concerned was acquired from another dealer or from a private collection which had to be broken up, so that in fact it originated not from an archaeological site, but from the house of a family, perhaps in Europe, who needed the money. There are no means of telling whether or not these explanations are true, but most museum officials are content to accept these propositions. The stranger, however, who turns up out of the blue with a choice bargain is treated in a much more suspicious manner, but even he, if he has the patience, will eventually sell what he has on offer.

One does not have to strain, however, except on behalf of the wealthy dealers, to appreciate the predicament in which everyone else involved is placed. The poor peasant who grubs a subsistence from parched fields is confronted with a temptation beyond the compass of most men's resistance when he finds on his doorstep what amounts to his own private oil well. At the other extreme, the progressive museum chief will finally have to face a great deal of criticism if he passes up a succession of dubious offers, only for them to appear elsewhere.

The whole essence of this problem was touched on on our arrival back in London. The brothers in Izmir had mentioned among the clients they named a dealer called Hugo Weissmann. He was, they alleged, someone who dealt with them regularly. If this were true, it became very important to make contact with him, especially since on our return we had discovered that the first two Hacilar pots bought by the British Museum had been obtained from Weissmann. It took a day to trace his telephone number and after some little persuasion he agreed to meet us at his flat.

Hugo Weissmann and his wife lived just off Baker Street in an apartment that most vividly proclaimed his profession. Almost every available flat surface in its rooms was used to display an antiquity. Precious vases and busts lined the walls in strategically decorative positions. Weissmann himself was an elderly figure of a nervous disposition who appeared as eager to discover what we knew as we were to question him. His wife, a dominant middle-European matron, seemed to be even more anxious to preserve their innocence.

We began by explaining what had been said about him in Izmir. He was quick to reject the allegations.

'It's not true at all,' he said passionately. 'I haven't been to Izmir for at least six years. In fact I retired from the business some time ago.'

'Then you don't do any more buying and selling?'

'Er . . . perhaps a little . . . if I hear about something from my friends.' He said this as would a man who had once played at Wimbledon but who, since his reactions had slowed down, now enjoyed a little tennis in a local park in the evenings just to keep his hand in.

'Then why should the men in Izmir mention your name?' we asked the retired dealer.

'You know what they are like,' he replied. 'They like to spread a few names about to keep up their prestige and to impress other customers.'

The conversation died. To keep it rolling, we asked about his background.

'I was born in Austria,' he said, 'and when the first world war started I became one of the youngest cavalry officers in the Emperor's Own First Hussars. Most of my fellow officers were aristocrats, and later on in my life they were of great help to me in my business. Over the years, some of them had things to sell. But that part of my life was also important for another reason. During the war I was transferred to Anatolia to act as a liaison officer to the Turks who were our allies. That is how I first got to know about the country.'

'Is it true that you sold the British Museum two of its Hacilar pots?'

'Er . . . what did you say?'

'The Hacilar pots in the British Museum. Is it true that they bought them from you?'

'Yes . . . yes, it is true. But who told you that?'

'It doesn't matter really, but we have been told this.' And since Weissmann was obviously off balance, it seemed the right moment to put in the next question. 'And what about the one in the Ashmolean museum in Oxford. You sold that one to them too?'

'The Ashmolean? Er . . . yes, I did.'

The confession was disturbing Mrs Weissmann. 'Pookie,' she said, 'you must be careful what you say. Please be careful.'

'But they know this already,' said Weissmann.

'Perhaps you would like to tell us where they came from in the first place?' we asked.

'Ah,' replied Weissmann, 'that is why the connections in my life are so important. They came from a collection on an estate in Austria near the Hungarian border.'

'What part of Austria exactly?'

'Please, please, you can't expect me to answer that. We dealers have to keep these places to ourselves. If I told you where, and it was printed, all the dealers in the world would descend on my friends and start to bargain with them.'

'In that case, perhaps you know how your friends acquired them in the first place?'

'Oh, that is easy,' said the dealer. 'Most of those objects came out of Turkey in 1938, long before export restrictions were imposed. And you must know that at that time no one in Europe knew what Hacilar painted pottery was. It may, up to that point, have been the first painted pottery in the world, but then no one had any idea that that was what it was. Some people thought it was pretty and collected it, and others, because no archaeologist had recorded its existence, thought it was fake and threw it away.'

Weissmann's explanation of this first appearance of the Hacilar material made sense. So many archaeologists jump to conclusions about the development patterns of their own particular fields, based solely on the known evidence, that when a discovery is made that throws doubts on their first theories, they are apt to be extremely sceptical of the value of the new information. The reasoning behind Weissmann's story about European reaction to the Hacilar artifacts had already been foreshadowed by a comment on Mellaart's Dorak discovery which reached us in a letter from Athens shortly after our return to London. An international dealer there, who was said to know something of the Dorak mystery, had been asked for his explanation of the disappearance of the treasure. This dealer, quite clearly, doubted that the find existed at all. We quote a section of the letter:

'The Dorak area has never yielded any Early Bronze Age antiquities of the so-called Yortan period (named after the village near Pergamum where the first Early Bronze Age relics were found). The alleged treasure was made up of a gold vase, part of a sword of Egyptian incrustations, silver statuettes and other valuables including embroideries. The materials are quite unlikely for that period. All that the Yortan period has yielded in Turkey has been black clay vases and a few marble idols. Otherwise, somewhere, somehow, similar objects would have turned up. These were so unique that they were improbable. . . .'

Apart from the strange logic of the dealer in Athens and his description of the Dorak material, which did not accord with Mellaart's report, he displayed the same scepticism as had the European collectors who rejected the first objects from Hacilar. Weissmann, obviously, knew the Anatolian field well. Perhaps he even knew how the Hacilar pots had been appearing on the international market in 1938?

'It was very simple then,' he said. 'In those days any parcel you were sending out of Turkey had to be taken to the post office open. They were only looking for gold, and when they saw that what you were wrapping up was only a pot, it was passed.'

'We accept your word, of course, that you were not involved in the smuggling, but perhaps you can tell us how the dealers operate there?'

'Be careful, please Pookie,' interrupted Mrs Weissmann.

'It's all right, my dear,' said the dealer. 'It won't do any harm to tell them that. One thing you must understand, the crooked dealers never carry any money and never carry the goods. They turn up in Izmir and make contact with the local merchants to see what they have got. The dealers in Izmir may tell them what they have to sell, but they never keep it in the shops. No, they'd never do that. What happens is that the visitor from abroad is taken by car to a house in the suburbs where the antiquities are kept. That way the police never find them. The buyer then looks the stuff over and says he'll take this, this and this. Then they bargain about the price. Once that is fixed, he tells them he will pay the money into an account in Switzerland as soon as he receives the goods.'

'They trust him then?'

'Oh, yes,' they will have been dealing with him for some time. You see, they do it that way, so that if the police should turn up at his hotel in Izmir and search his room, they won't find any extraordinary sums of money or any of the antiquities. It is all done on trust.'

'But how does he get the stuff out of Turkey?' we asked.

'You didn't hear about the Transporter while you were in Istanbul?'

'No. Who's that?'

Mrs Weissmann was growing agitated. 'Pookie, you must take care.'

'It's all right, my dear. I am telling them a lot I am sure they already know. Well, the dealer goes on to Istanbul and makes contact with the Transporter. He tells him that in Izmir at such-and-such an address he has some goods waiting to be shipped, say, to America. He tells the man, "I want them at this place by a certain date", and he flies home.'

'It's as easy as that?'

'This man can get anything out of Turkey. And not just through the post office. He must use other means. A little bit of bribery here and there. I know this is true. I know that he has been able to get out of the country Hellenistic bronze statues four feet high. And you don't do that through the post office.'

'Perhaps, then, you could tell us who the Transporter is? We've heard of one or two names that might fit the description.'

Mrs Weissmann leaned forward in her chair and clasped her hands together in an attitude of prayer.

'Pookie, Pookie, I beg of you, please do not tell these people the name of this man. You know what can happen to you. I beg of you. You know what happens to people who talk of these things.'

Hugo Weissmann hesitated for a second. 'But I want to help them.'

'It doesn't matter. They are nothing to you. Why should you put yourself in danger? I beg of you.'

Her husband thought for a moment. 'She is right. I cannot tell you. You mustn't ask me to tell you. You will see how dangerous it is, if I tell you what has happened in the past. You must believe me, but I know of three men who once talked about these things and they were all stabbed to death. You are smiling. I will tell you, it happened in Aleppo, Homs and Beirut.'

In fact, it was easy to smile at this sort of threat as the safe sound of London traffic brushed passed the open window, but, as Weissmann was relieved to discover, we sympathised with him. On at least two occasions recently in the comparatively modern world of antiques in Britain, frustrated dealers at an auction had threatened the highest bidder with violence. In one instance, they had crowded the successful buyer in such a way that the police had to be called; and in the other, the winner had returned to his car to find that all four wheels had been stolen and the vehicle rested on its axles in the street. If, in these relatively civilised surroundings, defeat could trigger off such passion, why, where tempers are less controlled, should not the knife be the settler of an argument?

'He was right you know.' Sitting on the other side of the lunch table was a young man in his late twenties, a member of one of London's biggest firms of auctioneers. Through his office there pass a great many valuable archaeological artifacts each year, to be knocked down under the hammer in front of an audience of some of the sharpest dealers in the world. The experience had somehow soured the young man and he was soon to leave his job to study archaeology as a profession. There is no doubt that whatever his firm did behind the auctioneer's rostrum was completely honest. It was the in-fighting that went on in front of it that he found disillusioning.

'He was right, you know,' he said. 'It was lucky that you were doing your story in Turkey and not in Persia. You stood a chance of getting a knife in you there.'

'You're joking, of course,' we said.

'Not in the least,' he replied. 'They're smuggling antique gold so fast out of Persia, it isn't true. There are a lot of things I've learnt since I've been in the job, but I can't tell you about them because of professional etiquette.'

'Do you happen to know anything about the sort of stuff

Mellaart's been digging up? Anything from Çatal Hüyük or Hacilar, for instance?' we asked him.

'I've never seen any objects on the market from Çatal Hüyük,' he replied, 'but I know a bit about Hacilar.'

'You've had some of that through your hands then?'

'Oh, there's been some, but the trouble is there's so much that is faked.'

'Do you mean to say that that gets into the auction rooms as well, with all those experts around?'

'Not if we can help it. Let me tell you what happened once in our place. A dealer came in with a box of stuff from Hacilar. You know, pots and the usual goddesses. He left them with us until the date of the auction. One day one of our men was shifting the stuff and he dropped it. Well, that's enough to make anyone go cold, but funnily enough it didn't turn out that way. We had a look at one of the broken goddesses and it had got pink dental plaster under the armpits. Well, when the dealer came back we told him we couldn't accept the lot for auction. I mean we didn't tell him what we thought, but he knew all right. He looked a bit green. I expect he bought them in good faith, but he had been landed with a load of fakes.'

'Have you got any idea of the proportion of fakes to the genuine article?'

'No, it's too difficult to tell, but I bet it's enormous. Not so long ago, a woman in the States was sold a Hacilar figure for £27,000 and you can bet your life that was a dud. It's bound to happen. There are so many people who want to get hold of the stuff, and they can change hands quite easily at £3,000 and above. Why shouldn't all those crooks try to make a quick profit. It's irresistible.'

'What do you think of the Dorak material then? Do you think that really existed?' we asked.

'I'm not sure,' said the young man, 'but while we've been talking I've been thinking of a solution to the mystery. It doesn't matter how odd you think it is, I can tell you from what I've seen that it could happen. Something like it has been done before.'

'Before you do that,' we interrupted, 'let's go over all the possibilities, and then we can see how your theory fits in.'

'All right,' he said. 'What do you think?'

At the top of the list, we told him, was the idea that the whole Dorak story as related by Mellaart was true, but that the archaeologist had refrained from giving anyone all the facts. He had somehow stumbled across the treasure, some-how got permission to record it, and then kept quiet about his discovery until tipped off that it had been smuggled out of the country. This is what the Turkish newspapers clearly believe. That thesis, however, raised a host of questions. Why did the owners in Izmir hold on to the Dorak material for so long? Why wait from 1922 until 1958 to remove this very hot collection from Turkey? Ah, the Turks would say, but it was not excavated during our War of Independence. It was uncovered at Dorak when we said it was: in 1955 or 1956. And, according to the Istanbul reporters, it was done then by Mellaart and a woman.

In that case, one must discount all the evidence in the police dossier at Mustafakemalpasha, believe that on oath the peasants in the village lied in their affidavits, cross off the evidence we had heard from the town journalist Ibrahim Erbek as unworthy of consideration, and examine the next set of probabilities. If the first contention were true, Mellaart would have been cut in on the profits. But there are no signs that he enjoys a standard of living above that of an ordinary university lecturer, beyond the benefits he derives from his marriage to a Turk whose family is comfortably off. More-over, he would have laid himself wide open to blackmail. There is little doubt that all the wiles of an academic, devious as some of them are, would be no match for a gang of astute crooks. At any time in the future they could have descended on Mellaart looking for help with the next coup. In addition, there is the question of the identity of the woman who was seen in the Dorak area with the man alleged to be Mellaart. It could not have been Anna Papastrati. She was much too young to fit the description. It could hardly have been Arlette Mellaart. She has no scars under her eyes and no gold teeth. This theory does not stand up under close examination.

The second proposition on the list toyed with the idea that the entire business was a hoax. Mellaart had invented all the incidents, fabricated the sketches, and written up his 'discovery' in an attempt to raise his prestige in the eyes of his colleagues. It must be remembered that Mellaart had first gone to Turkey with the idea at the back of his head that perhaps the mysterious Sea People, who roamed the Eastern Mediterranean around 1200 B.C., had originally stemmed from the coasts of Asia Minor. How convenient it would be subsequently to run across an archaeological bonanza which revealed hitherto unknown information about a kingdom of people who lived by a lake which was connected with the Sea of Marmara. A sword blade among the uncovered material even carried a decoration of sea-going ships.

This theory first of all presupposes that Mellaart was in desperate need for prestige among his colleagues. But, in fact, in 1958 he was well on the way to promoting his own future at Hacilar. There already lay behind him a reputation for homing like a mine-detector on valuable objects buried in the earth; and it is scarcely possible that he had first put them there himself. Where would he have got them from? Moreover, it is one thing to pull off a Piltdown Man fake by bringing together disparate elements of a skull, and fooling the rest of the world into thinking that they belonged to one hominid; but that is a far cry from establishing the genuineness of the Dorak material by similar methods. That would have meant first of all concocting a story of its discovery which the world would believe; and it would not take much literary flair to improve on the girl-on-the-train idea. Then inventing an entire range of sketches which satisfied one's colleagues, as it had done both in Turkey and in England, that this is how the things looked. And then to write a 60,000-word text, every aspect of which rang true. Fixing the Piltdown bones may have meant a night or two in an amateur laboratory, but forging the Dorak ambience would have been the work of months. And where could this have taken place? In a house swarming with people not privy to the secret? Where else then? And if the whole incident was one of fantastic invention, why would a man complicate his life unnecessarily by composing a letter from a girl that suggested that they had been on the friendliest terms. 'If it was a hoax,' says Dr Barnett, head of Western Asiatic Antiquities at the British Museum, who was interviewed on the subject, 'it would be the greatest hoax ever perpetrated in the history of archaeology.' It is reasonably safe to discount this theory too.

The third explanation springs from the suggestion made by Hüseyin Taluy, ex-chief of police of Izmir. It was he who thought the girl on the train was a deliberate plant to make contact with Mellaart and then to lead him to the treasure in the house. What girl, the police captain had asked, would identify herself to a stranger over the Dorak discovery without any certainty that he would not betray her? What girl, in fact, would get on a train in Turkey wearing an immensely valuable bracelet of the period of Troy without risking unwanted attention? It follows therefore that Anna Papastrati, if that was her name, knew who she was talking to from the very beginning. And if that was the case, what was her purpose? According to Kadri Cenani, Mellaart's father-in-law, Taluy had told him that Ankara might be involved. The inference was that certain members of Turkey's Department of Antiquities had wished to discredit the English archaeologist through feelings of jealousy. It is true that the ex-chief of police had not positively affirmed this idea when the ques-

tion was put to him again in Izmir; but he had not denied it
either. But whatever Byzantine emotions lurk in the psy-
chology of some of Turkey's own archaeologists, there would
have been easier ways of trapping Mellaart than this. Plant-
ing a valuable artifact in his baggage and then alerting
Customs to discover it, would have done the trick. There was
no guarantee, for instance, that Mellaart, once picked up,
would follow the girl across the bay to Karşiyaka. The plot,
if it were a plot, was too vulnerable for scheming bureaucrats
to risk. This third theory, however, was the suggestion of a
police executive who can be judged to know something of
the way of crooks. If his tentative conclusions can be dismissed, is there not something to be said for his initial idea?
Our companion that day in London, the erstwhile auctioneer,
thought so.

'But I'll give you an ending to his story that makes more
sense,' he said. 'I agree with your police chief that the girl
was planted on the train to bring Mellaart into the net, but it
wasn't operated from Ankara. You've no idea what lengths
some dealers will go to to make a killing on the international
market. I've heard of things like this before. It could have
been the work of a gang that was out for a big profit. The
girl fits into the picture exactly as you'd imagine. These gangs
always work with a girl like that. Now, what I imagine
happened was this. Someone had got hold of a few genuine
objects of the Yortan culture from, say, around Dorak, but
these alone wouldn't be enough to bring in a fat prize. So,
with the help of some other dealers from Greece or Egypt,
they would begin to add a few items which developed the
picture a bit more. You know, add the gold leaf from the
throne to give the collection a date. On top of that they'd
bring some other stuff from outside, and some of that could
be fake. Now, you've built up a collection and a story that
begins to make sense, but what you need then is someone
who's going to give the whole thing authenticity. Well, if

they were playing about with that period, Mellaart would be their man. It would be the easiest thing in the world to check his movements and to find out what he was doing. They'd know soon enough that he was going to make a train trip to Izmir, and at the right spot the girl would get on the train. The rest you know.'

'But would a man like Mellaart fall for it?'

'It would be a very rare bird who didn't. Don't forget the atmosphere he was working in. He's let into this secret, which is enough to excite anyone; and then he's told that he can't take photographs but that he can make sketches. So he has to work hard against a time limit that he sets in his own mind —the fact that at any moment she might appear to get frightened by the whole thing and whip everything out of sight. It's an old trick in this business to dangle the bait. You know, you show someone something good and then say that you're very sorry you can't let them buy it, but it's already promised to someone else, or it's got to be cleaned first and then revalued, and so on. . . . The fish is jumping to bite.'

'But how would they use him then?'

'Oh, they probably had a potential buyer in mind already. You see what happens—Mellaart goes away, while they hold on to the stuff and shift it to another house. They wait for him to publish his findings; then the whole world knows about it. His stamp on it gives it authenticity and a price on the world market, and by that time it's out of the country and slap into the lap of some crazy millionaire. They share out the profits and split up. They probably made a fortune.'

'And Mellaart carries the can.'

'Precisely.'

This fourth theory, it must be said, does account for every aspect of the affair in spite of its James Bond ring. In a world in which, one had come to learn over the past few weeks, faking, thieving, jealousy, smuggling, distortion and be- trayal are the currency of some amateur archaeologists and professional dealers, such a thesis would have its roots nourished to perfection. There remained, of course, Mellaart himself and his reaction to the fourth conclusion. He was contacted on the Bosphorus and the facts related to him, mention even being made that some of the material may have been faked. Mellaart's only response was to agree: it could have been that way, he said.

But where does that leave Turkey? With a coastline that is open to four seas, it is clear that once a priceless artifact is in the hands of the crooks there is little that the authorities can do about it. The routes out of the country are well established. How else can the comparatively wealthy museums of the world still continue to acquire the nation's riches? And where the dealers, Turk and foreign, run up against the law, what resistance to bribery can local forces erect in an economy that can only afford to pay its servants a minimum wage?

The answer is, of course, not to appeal to international co-operation, but for Turkey to put its own house in order. When the Turks are asked why they do not guard all their most important archaeological sites, they point to the cost of doing so. But this is an economic fallacy: the value of what is being lost each year would pay for a comprehensive security service ten times over. Its laws which govern the handling of antiquities are of little help. Turkey's almost complete prohibition of their export merely exaggerates the shortage of supply; and this is a shortage which individuals or gangs will remedy by smuggling or forgery.

There is an example from which Turkey could learn. In Egypt, for example, mixed committees of nationals and foreigners examine the results of each season's excavations to decide which artifacts should remain in the country and which may be taken abroad. In this way, what is unique is kept at home where it belongs, while some of the rest is allowed to find its way to museums overseas. And students all the world over, who may be unable to travel, are thus brought into direct contact with the material evidence of the periods they study. In this way, too, the alien archaeologist is made to feel recompensed for his labours. There is, as a result, little frustration to provoke him into hazardous acts.

In the meantime, one may ask, is Turkey, with more immediately important political problems to be settled, sufficiently aware of the urgent need to tackle this one? One wonders. Our first account of the Mellaart affair was published in the *Sunday Times* in London in a two-part series at the beginning of November 1966. It seemed to us, however others may disagree with its implications, that it had been based on fact as far as that was discernible. We could hardly expect that the Turkish Press would fall over itself with joy; but at least, one hoped, if it were to demolish the results of our research, it would do so on the basis of evidence which clearly contradicted our own. It was a false hope. The result was a storm. While the sculptured leopards at Çatal Hüyük could change their spots with the advent of each new shrine, the newspapers of Ankara and Istanbul were incapable of such a transformation.

An exit for the U.S. Army Post Office in Izmir, where, dealers in Istanbul said, any antique artifact could be shipped out of the country without passing through Turkish Customs

At Kanlica on the Bosphorus, James Mellaart, with his Turkish wife, Arlette, and his father-in-law, Kadri Cenani

Chapter 11

The Aftermath

The Turks were not slow to move. Before the second article on the Dorak mystery had a chance to be published in Britain, the London representative of the Turkish newspaper *Yeni Gazete* ('The New Gazette') was on the phone.

'I am most interested in what you have been writing in your magazine, could I come along and talk to you about it?' he asked.

It would have been churlish to refuse. There was always the chance that there was at least one Turkish journalist who was keen to examine the evidence without a built-in bias that clouded his brain; and so we invited him to the 'The Blue Lion', a pub near the office which has become an annexe to its operations. He had great charm and was most eager to buy his share of food and drinks. The theme of his conversation, however, had a familiar ring. What was the second article on smugglers really about?

'If you are able to identify some of the men in my country who steal these things,' he said, 'you can imagine how interested we are to print the facts.'

'Naturally,' we replied, 'but then so are a lot of your friends. That's all they were after in Istanbul, but like them you'll have to wait.'

'But I do not want to take from you what you know. I can negotiate on behalf of my paper to buy what you have written. Can I not see the magazine?'

We thought for a moment, and then said, 'Well, that's a decision that only the editor of the magazine can make. Come across the road with us and we will ask him.'

But while we waited in the entrance hall for the lift to take us to the fourth floor, the Turkish journalist began to suggest things which carried an altogether different connotation.

'You know,' he said, 'if you let me have this information it will be much better for you.'

'How do you mean?'

'Well, my paper is one of the best in Turkey, and if we print the story as you wrote it, it will be much safer for you if you ever go back again.'

'Much safer?'

'I mean, you cannot always rely on what the other papers will say, and that could mean trouble.'

'You aren't by any chance trying to blackmail us into giving you this material?'

It was, he said, the last thing in his mind.

The editor of the *Sunday Times* colour magazine, introduced to the fact that here was a potential buyer of some of his material, was courteous enough to allow the Turk to see an advance copy of the next issue. It was good, said the Turk, and what would he have to do to acquire the rights to run it in his country? The operation was simple: he was introduced to the member of the staff who dealt with syndication. They discussed the matter for some fifteen minutes and a price was negotiated; as a result of which, the Turk walked out of the office with the magazine under his arm on two conditions: he would contact his office in Turkey by phone and agree the price, and in the event of a deal no part of the article would appear in his newspaper until after the next Sunday, the day of our own publication. It was the last that was seen of him.

On Saturday, 12 November, 1966, *Yeni Gazete*'s front page carried the story across all its columns, the day before the article was due to appear in Britain. The betrayal of trust was one thing—something which one could only accept as a hazard of this kind of dealing: but the slanted implications of the extracts put another colour on the facts. First of all, it implied, it was our magazine which alleged that Mellaart was involved in smuggling. This was said as if *Milliyet* had never existed. It was then noted that the artifacts the archaeologist had excavated had been removed from Turkey, which was patently not true. Furthermore, Şevket Çetinkaya was described not only as an ex-chauffeur, but as a man 'who was employed by Mellaart as a driver'. This again was a clear distortion of what had been stated. Try as one might to accept the twists in the story as the complications of translation, it was apparent, as misconception followed misconception, that this was more than a problem of linguistics. Once again, the narrative was being bent to find the ultimate scapegoat. Whole passages of the story were condensed into single defamatory sentences. 'We have focused attention on the smugglers' route from Hacilar', ran one, 'because of its association with Mellaart'. Of course, we had focused attention on the route from Hacilar, because that is where the local villagers had tried to sell us some of its pots and because that was the site from which Çetinkaya had made his fortune. But *Yeni Gazete*'s account of our story was not satisfied with just 'borrowing' the text; it was also liberally illustrated with photographs lifted straight from the magazine.

The following day, the Sunday, *Yeni Gazete* covered its version of the story with a headline that inadvertently told the truth. 'The Allegations Made by the *Sunday Times*', it proclaimed, 'Caused Confusion amongst the Antique Dealers.' Since this was a section of the community with which we had little sympathy, its message was one which could stand unchallenged. The next headline, 'The Police Possess Many Undisclosed Documents', could only refer to the Dorak dossier and imply that Turkish journalists had so far been unable to examine its contents. So far so good. But the third deck implied a thought which was as damning of the newspaper's attitude as one could ever find. 'The Antique Dealers', it said, 'Are not in favour of allowing Foreign Archaeologists to enter the Country'. As if, in a serious consideration of this problem, the men who traded in illegally acquired artifacts could have any influence in solving it. The text that followed was even more bizarre. Hüseyin Kocabaş was supposed to have looked at the photograph of the dealer in the Covered Bazaar with the Hacilar goddess he had on offer, and identified it at once as a fake. 'There are hardly eight or ten real idols on the surface of the earth,' he is quoted as saying. 'One can, however, find thousands of fakes. Owing to the persistence of tourists, and in order to give something and make money, even the villagers themselves are making goddesses and selling them at whatever price they can obtain.' Precisely.

The next section of the Turkish article confirmed Kocabaş' allegations. It also acted as an illuminating introduction to the tune that was to be sung by other Turkish newspapers in the next two or three weeks. *Yeni Gazete*'s Istanbul reporter had run to earth the dealer in the bazaar. He was then interviewed. 'I remember that man and woman,' he said. 'They also had an interpreter with them.' (We did not. His own assistant spoke fluent English) 'I did not ask 300 dollars as a price.' (He did.) 'Suppose I had a goddess I wanted to sell, would I ask 300 dollars for an antique worth 30 dollars?' (But of course he had.) What followed is hardly worth analysing except for his conclusion, which speaks for itself and is a warning to anyone who shops in the Covered Bazaar. 'Every antique has its fakes,' he finished, 'and we are merely selling the fakes. . . .'

But as the newspaper's second article moved towards its summing-up, in the words of another dealer we had not met, it delivered a real *cri de cœur*. This man, described as a colonel, talked of the Byzantine silver which is now in America. 'Even the police know about this,' he said. 'There is a file connected with this case. The Government, the Foreign Ministry must take up the case and ask for its return.... Thus at least other smugglers of antiquities will be discouraged. The British are right on this score.' It was a relief to know that at least.

Having first launched itself on an examination of the state of smuggling in Turkey by way of our own report, however, *Yeni Gazete* on the Monday began to make its own contribution to the subject. In a column headlined 'Thoughts', its editor, in locally poetic fashion, set up his contention: 'There is no doubt that our subterranean and submarine treasures do not consist only of copper, chromium, oil and fish. One of the treasures which is of equal importance to these consists of the antiquities and ancient monuments of Asia Minor.... From the statue of Venus smuggled from the Island of Milos down to the stone remains of Troy, thousands of antiquities which fill up the museums of Berlin, London and Paris have all been carried there from Turkey. We thought with the coming of the Republic the monkey would wake up. However, our eyes are still closed, and closed very tightly for that matter....'

In the same issue of this newspaper, a leading article persisted with the theme in the same vein. 'Information given to us by foreigners about the way we are robbed of our antiquities has grieved many collectors.... It is impossible not to receive their sorrow with sincerity and not to share in this. However, to listen to what foreigners say about ourselves and to shed tears is, contrary to what the poet says, crying for our own ridiculous state of affairs.... Turkey is like an unguarded treasure. Moreover, all the nations of the world consider stealing from this treasure as legal.... There is an old law which is meant to safeguard antiquities. However, this law, which is not even capable of meeting the conditions of its time, is at present so full of deficiencies and so ridiculous that it needs to be removed from the shelf of the very antiquities that it is supposed to protect. . . . Although a new project has been ready for many years, yet the present law has not been allowed to be cast into the past. And even if there were no evil intentions lurking in the background, the new project has not managed to climb over the wall of indolence and bureaucracy. . . .' One can but sympathise, even though one recognises that such a new law would be a bad law and ultimately circumvented. After all, although once a law decreed that all male babies of the Hebrews should be put to death, Moses was still discovered hidden in the bullrushes.

Nevertheless, in spite of its distortions, *Yeni Gazete* had tried to state a case. Not so *Milliyet*, which by 27 November was once again on the warpath. Turhan Aytul, who had originally dedicated himself to the task of chasing Mellaart, on that day began a second crusade with a prefatory article setting up as a target his eternal Aunt Sally. It was, as usual, a piece of writing that existed in its own world. Nothing that had taken place before, that smacked of concrete evidence, seemed to carry any weight with this myopic reporter. His preface started off in a blaze of glory. 'Mellaart,' said the headline, 'has been removed from the British Institute of Archaeology.' (He had, it is true, because of the temper of his letter to Toronto, been rejected by the Board of the Institute as a member whom it would back to apply to excavate in Turkey; but this was not the same thing as removing him from the Institute.) The headline, however, was a mere aperitif to the misquotations and misconceptions which ensued. They would stretch from here back to prehistory. 'Mellaart', we are supposed to have said, 'had nothing to do with the case'. The Royal treasure of Dorak, he went on, is one of the oldest and most important treasures of history. (In theory, perhaps.) It is extremely difficult to read

what Aytul had written without interpolating a counter-
balancing comment at the end of almost every sentence. 'This
great robbery which took place between 1955–58. . . .' Aytul
repeated the old charges without quoting the evidence and
had this time extended the dates. And he had now grown
even more emphatic: '. . . the British archaeologist James
Mellaart who is the No. 1 man of the Dorak robbery. . . .'
Outside Turkey, of course, such a statement would have even
the laziest of lawyers reaching for his telephone to suggest a
small libel suit. But Aytul is not one to be dismayed.
'Mellaart,' he added, 'in view of the nasty attitude against
him by the Institute to which he belonged, strived to save the
situation by using the medium of the Press.' (Apart from the
fact that the reporter's time scale is completely wrong, there
has not been one instance of the archaeologist contacting his
own or American newspapers.)

Turhan Aytul's next accusation steps outside all the realms
of probability. 'At the beginning of 1966,' he says, 'Mellaart
came to Turkey with Joseph Allsop [sic], one of the cele-
brated journalists of the *New York Herald Tribune*, and
stayed for fifteen days. However, Joseph Allsop did not write
anything about this matter in spite of the archaeologist's
request.' This is too easy to refute. In the first place Alsop
did not journey to Turkey with Mellaart. Secondly, before
the American arrived in Istanbul, Mellaart had asked for and
received Ankara's approval to take the writer to Çatal
Hüyük. And thirdly, as for the allegation that the Washington reporter was contacted by the archaeologist, it is best to
leave the journalist to record the facts. They came in response
to a letter we had sent to the States, and it read:

'I write to you to say that my trip with Mellaart in Turkey
was entirely my idea. I had been immensely struck by the
profound importance of his great discovery at Çatal Hüyük,
and I wanted to write about it for *The New Yorker*. Quite
out of the blue, I therefore proposed a *New Yorker* article on

Çatal Hüyük to Mellaart, using previous archaeological articles I had done for that magazine in lieu of an introduction. With great kindness, he consented to assist me. I am now working on the article, which will cover not only Çatal Hüyük, but also a good many of the other astonishing additions that have recently been made to our knowledge of the origins of civilisation in the Neolithic period. Although I sympathise with him, I don't intend to touch upon Mellaart's difficulties with the Turkish archaeological authorities; for these have nothing to do with my real subject, which is what is now called the Neolithic revolution.

'Mellaart not only made no attempt whatever to persuade me to write about his dispute with the Turkish archaeological service; he also made no attempt whatever to persuade me to write about Çatal Hüyük. The whole expedition that we took together, as I have said, was entirely my idea. I doubt indeed whether Mellaart had ever heard of me before I wrote to him, and anyone who accuses Mellaart of "persuading me to write about him in America" is a malicious liar.'

Joseph Alsop's letter was reassuring. It proved to us at least that our own reading of *Milliyet*'s attitude was not distorted by any emotional bias towards a compatriot. In fact, Turhan Aytul's allegations were too remote from the truth to bother with except, as in the past, they coloured opinion not only in Turkey but also among some archaeologists in Europe. His next paragraph, in his introduction, for example, trod an even more easily refuted line. 'In spite of the fact that the said series of articles [ours] were written in order to influence the decision to be taken in connection with Mellaart by the British Archaeological Institute, whose head office is in London; yet, the High Tribunal, which met under the chairmanship of the former British ambassador, Sir James Bowler [it is Bowker], removed Mellaart from the Institute.' It was gratifying to learn that we were being credited with the gift of prophecy: no such decision to censor Mellaart (not in these extreme terms as it happens) was taken until after our return to England.

But, as we were to discover by the third of Aytul's series of nine inflammatory articles, we were not the only ones to be favoured with this intuition of foresight. In reporting what was alleged to be our description of the Dorak hoard, Turhan Aytul had invested this strange people with a knowledge unprecedented in history. 'The tomb stones', we are supposed to have written, 'had been discovered near the Dorak village. They were the relics of the Yortan culture and belonged to the state of Troy. *On one of the stones the date 3000 B.C. was inscribed*'. This of course implied that not only did the Yortan race know that Christ was going to be born, but when as well. If a reporter can make this sort of error, even in translation—since that would be his excuse, it is safe to assume that his approach to more disputable facts will be even more irresponsible.

We will resist the temptation to catalogue even further the mistakes, intentional and unintentional, that flow through the rest of his writing. After that remarkable gaffe, the exercise would be meaningless. But there is one more aspect of his own so-called investigation which carried much more sinister overtones. They impart a nightmarish quality in retrospect to our journey through Anatolia; as though during the trip we had been operating on a plane once removed from reality. Our account, in the first place, was described by Turhan Aytul as 'a wolf's tale'; this we presumed, while admiring the phrase, meant that it was a pack of lies. But it is what followed, to substantiate his allegations, which gives his own series this other-planet theme. For almost all our own witnesses, people that we intentionally interviewed as a team to check on each other's impressions, and whose words were further witnessed by expert interpreters, almost all of them are made to recant on what they said.

This peculiar element in the *Milliyet* series begins with the evidence of Zeki Küneralp, once the Turkish ambassador in London and now head of the Foreign Office civil service in Ankara. 'Zeki Küneralp,' writes Aytul, 'never said to Mellaart in London, "Who is your enemy in Ankara? Find him!"' And that's the statement; as bald as that. There is no mention of who made this counter-claim. No hint of where it was made. Not even the merest suggestion that Küneralp denied the whole thing himself. Nothing. Just a flat denial.

The second instance describes very strange circumstances in which we are supposed to have met Hüseyin Taluy, the ex-chief of police, in Izmir. The following are said to be the opening questions put to him by us:

'We want to talk to you about the Mellaart affair. Mellaart is not an archaeologist. Somehow he obtained permission to dig at Alacahüyük, and he carried out excavations here. As he is incapable of valuating the antiquities he found, he sent these to London, where their values have been assessed. It is said that these are valuable discoveries. Later on he published a description of these in the *Illustrated London News*. Now we belong to a rival newspaper and we want to ask you: Do not the actions of Mellaart constitute a crime? Why don't you arrest and imprison him?'

Apart from the fact that the comic-opera quality of this speech is very amusing, and could be dismissed as bearing so little relation to the truth as to be worthless, it is disturbing to find even a policeman of Taluy's high rank contributing to the confusion of facts. Even from internal evidence, that supposed speech can be reduced to shreds. Who in the world could say that Mellaart is not an archaeologist? What is he supposed to be doing, digging at Alacahüyük, a pre-Hittite site in Anatolia far removed in time and space from Mellaart's field? Who could say, without fear of libelling the man, that he was incapable of evaluating archaeological artifacts? How can the *Sunday Times* representatives describe themselves as rivals of the *Illustrated London News*, a picture magazine owned by the same proprietor? And finally, what person who laid the faintest claim to being an objective observer would wind up his opening set of questions with two as loaded as those?

Even Ibrahim Erbek, the journalist of Mustafakemalpasha is made to go back on his interview with us in the local police station. In fact, Turhan Aytul produced from him in front of a notary the following statement:

'In 1962 when I saw Mellaart's photograph in *Milliyet*, I recognised it and told Turhan Aytul "this is Mellaart".

'This is how I came to know Mellaart: In 1956—this is approximately—they came to Mustafakemalpasha in a jeep. They said they were geologists and that they were searching for coal. At that time I was the proprietor of the *Ataeli* newspaper. The woman who was with Mellaart has a great resemblance to the picture published in the *Sunday Times*, which Turhan Aytul showed me today. They asked me in English and in French whether I spoke English and French. When I said "No", they talked to each other in English. Whereupon I scoffed at them by asking whether they were subjecting the Anatolian journalist to examination; because the woman knew Turkish. But her accent was not that of a Turk, but that of a non-Moslem. After ascertaining whether I knew other languages or not, they procured the opportunity of talking to each other in comfort.

'They told me they had come for coal prospecting. We informed them that there were rich coal mines in Devecikonak. But they insisted on going to Söğütalan. I asked a youth of Söğütalan to accompany them. This friend took them to Söğütalan. They are said to have left the youth there and to have gone to Dorak. At Dorak they are said to have seen the head of the village and to have told him that they wanted to go to the Cemetery of the non-Moslems. They are said to have gone there accompanied by some labourers, in search of coal.

'It is said that on their return they paid the men between 15–20 liras each in wages. Afterwards I found out from the villagers that they had also given 100 liras to the headman. Naturally this news was given to me because I was a journalist. Recently an English journalist came here in connection with this affair. They were examining the dossier in the Public Prosecutor's Office. As my name was involved in the affair, they asked to see me, too. I talked to them through an interpreter. In the analysis of the types they were, as if, trying to impose their views on me.

'I don't know what is going to appear in the English newspaper attributed to me. I only talked to the interpreter. What I told is exactly the same as the statement I am giving to Turhan Aytul. I must add, however, that Mellaart is concealing the reason why he came to Mustafakemalpasha and does not wish to confront us before the Turkish Courts of Law.'

We have given Erbek's most recent statement in full, at the risk of covering the same ground again, in order to give the Turkish journalists the fullest opportunity to express their own views. But as with Taluy's own account of our investigations, Erbek seems to have been present at a different interview. The questions are obvious. Would Mellaart's Turkish wife, if it were she, ask a fellow Turk if he spoke other languages, in those languages, unless it was to test him out? And would he know enough of those languages to say he didn't speak them? Furthermore, why should Arlette Mellaart, if it were she, not be speaking in a Turkish accent, unless her upbringing modified the way she handled her own language? According to Erbek's statement to us, the couple had been advised by the journalist himself to go to Söğütalan for coal. It is also worth questioning the validity of the second half of his latest statement. Do Turkish notaries accept as valid, statement after statement based only on hearsay, as the continually repeated phrase 'they are said to

have . . .' indicates? And how could we have possibly asked
to see Erbek when we were not aware of his existence until he
walked into the prosecutor's office uninvited by us? On the
other hand, if we appeared to be trying to impose our views
on him, we can only apologise. It is not the way we believe
the interview was conducted. As for the fact that the interrogation was carried on through an interpreter, it is enough to
point out that our translator, a member of the staff of the
Turkish Ministry of Tourism, spoke fluent and perfect
English, and that as we were aware of the dangers involved,
Erbek was taken over and over again through his most salient
points.

But it would be futile to go on examining Turkish accounts
of the Mellaart affair detail by detail. We believe we have
repeated enough of their efforts to show once again the sloppy
manner in which they conducted their own investigations,
the suggestive undertones of their writings, and the freedom
they enjoy to libel a man with little fear of legal retaliation.
It has often been asked in the past why Mellaart has never
made any attempt to seek some redress in the Turkish courts,
nor at least tried to put his own point of view to the Turkish
newspapers. The answer is simple. In the first place, he has
been continually advised by both Turkish and British colleagues to let things ride in the hope that the hue and cry
would die down. After our own recent experiences in trying
to refute in Turkey the allegations made against ourselves, it
is easier to understand how impossible this is. In sheer
desperation one feels, his agreement to tell us his story was
the only answer.

Mellaart's experiences since then have not been the hap-
piest. In the autumn of 1966, the Council of the Institute of
Archaeology in London met to consider what action it should
take over the offensive passages that appeared in his letter to
Toronto. Mellaart was asked to leave that meeting when he
had given his view of the affair, and he waited in an ante-

room for some time while raised voices in the distance debated the issue. In the end the Council agreed to disassociate itself from backing his applications to excavate in Turkey. It meant, for the time being at least, that Mellaart could not return to his one great passion—Çatal Hüyük. Today, instead, regardless of the overblown accounts of the Council's measure given in the press of Istanbul and Ankara, Mellaart is still a member of the Institute's Council, still belongs to the Institute itself, and lectures regularly in the School of Archaeology. He even lectures in other parts of the University of London, and elsewhere in the city, on occasions when these events are crowned with the supreme irony. Almost invariably these talks are attended by representatives from the Turkish Embassy in London, and almost invariably Mellaart is congratulated by these foreign visitors on the success of his work.

Two things remain. On 24 November, 1966, Mehmet Ali Birand, *Milliyet*'s own diplomatic correspondent who was present at the first interview with Turhan Aytul in his office and later at the final questioning of Mellaart at Kanlica, wrote from Istanbul. 'Your articles were very well studied,' he said. 'I must congratulate you.'

And finally, when our first articles had been prepared for publication in London, a message reached us in the office that Sir Bernard Burrows of the Foreign Office would not be averse to a chat with us. There seemed no reason why we should not agree to a meeting, especially as it might prove instructive for us. Sir Bernard was then Deputy Under-Secretary for State and is now Permanent United Kingdom Representative to NATO in Paris.

Sir Bernard, who was the British Ambassador in Ankara at the time when Mellaart was working there, explored a familiar theme: the advisability of publishing the articles at all in the light of their possible repercussions. His tact was that of the perfect diplomat. Nevertheless, we found ourselves once again having to explain the reasons for our investigations.

'What would you do?' we asked. 'There is a balance. On one side there is the accumulated weight of a long series of accusations which have blackened the reputation of one man without, whatever one might assume personally, a single shred of evidence being brought to light to support them. Do you not think that our research would have been totally unnecessary if at an earlier stage the British Institute in Ankara had sought either to clear the name of one of its members, or somehow to investigate the allegations themselves? And on the other side sits the integrity of one man. We're not trying to defend him. We have just looked at the facts.'

Sir Bernard nodded. 'I see what you mean.'

We left Whitehall, wondering if he did.